KRISTI MCLELLAND

Jesus & Women

Lifeway Press®
Brentwood, Tennessee

Published by Lifeway Press® • © 2022 Kristi McLelland

Reprinted March 2023

ISBN: 978-1-0877-7395-7

Item: 005839466

Dewey decimal classification: 248.843

Subject heading: JESUS CHRIST / WOMEN / MIDDLE EAST / BIBLE—SOCIAL LIFE AND CUSTOMS

To order additional copies of this resource, write Lifeway Resources Customer Service; 200 Powell Place, Suite 100; Brentwood, TN 37027; Fax order to 615.251.5933; call toll-free 800.458.2772; email orderentry@lifeway.com; or order online at www.lifeway.com.

Printed in the United States of America.

Lifeway Women Bible Studies
Lifeway Resources
200 Powell Place, Suite 100
Brentwood, TN 37027

**EDITORIAL TEAM
LIFEWAY WOMEN
BIBLE STUDIES**

Becky Loyd
Director

Michelle Hicks
Manager

Sarah Doss
Content Editor

Erin Franklin
Production Editor

Lauren Ervin
Graphic Designer

Micah Kandros Design
Cover Designer

TABLE OF CONTENTS

ABOUT THE AUTHOR

Kristi McLelland is a speaker, teacher, and college professor. Since completing her Masters of Arts in Christian Education at Dallas Theological Seminary, she has dedicated her life to discipleship, to teaching people how to study the Bible for themselves, and to writing about how God is better than we ever knew by explaining the Bible through a Middle Eastern lens. Her great desire for people to truly experience the love of God birthed a ministry in which she leads biblical study trips to Israel, Turkey, Greece, and Italy.

For more information about Kristi and what she's up to, visit: NewLensBiblicalStudies.com.

INTRODUCTION

"A BIBLE WITH ITS JEWISHNESS WRUNG OUT OF IT IS NO BIBLE. A CHRIST WITH HIS JEWISHNESS OBSCURED IS NO CHRIST AT ALL."[1]
—DR. RUSSELL MOORE

Every adventure begins in a moment, and the best ones come to us. In 2007 an adventure found me. The Lord opened the door for me to go study the Bible in Egypt and Israel.

At the time, I was teaching Bible in the Biblical Studies department at Williamson College. I went to the Middle East in a spirit of professional development, just to learn, but God had other plans—much better plans.

In Israel I was amazed to see how different the Middle Eastern culture was and is from our Western culture. I started noticing how I was approaching the Bible as a Westerner, seeing it with Western eyes and asking Western questions of the biblical text. In Israel I learned the Bible through a cultural lens, the Middle Eastern lens.

In these early days of my Middle Eastern study, God totally and thoroughly wrecked me in the best of ways. He completely transformed me.

Learning the Bible in its original historical, cultural, linguistic, and geographic context allowed me to get to know Jesus in *His* Jewish world. I didn't just fly over to Israel; it felt almost as if I went back in time to learn about the first-century world of the Bible, the world Jesus lived in two thousand years ago.

"WE HAVE FORGOTTEN THAT WE READ THE BIBLE AS FOREIGNERS, AS VISITORS WHO HAVE TRAVELED NOT ONLY TO A NEW GEOGRAPHY BUT A NEW CENTURY. WE ARE LITERARY TOURISTS WHO ARE DEEPLY IN NEED OF A GUIDE."[2]
—GARY M. BURGE

You may be wondering about the meaning behind the cover of our study. The vessel pictured there is a tear jar, an actual archaeological artifact dating back to the first or second century AD. It was uncovered in Israel where one of my professors gave it to me as a gift.

This tear jar most likely belonged to a Jewish woman in antiquity, maybe even in the lifetime of Jesus' earthly ministry. In the ancient Near East, Jewish women collected their tears in a tear jar and poured them out to God in worship as a sign of faith, embodying God's message in Psalm 56:8 where He says He keeps our tears in a bottle. I look at the tear jar often and wonder what the original owner's story might have looked like—what she experienced, her highs and lows. I wonder where she kept her jar and how often she pulled it out to collect her tears before the Lord.

To me, the tear jar represents some of what the woman in Jesus' first-century world would have experienced. She was not always valued by society; she was often marginalized in the culture of the day. And yet God saw her grief and her struggle. He encouraged her to bring the pain to Him in worship and prayer. And, then, in Jesus, He worked to restore woman and show her His redemptive purposes in her life. He valued her; He lifted her up out of shame. He set her on the path to life. And He desires to do the same for you and for me, as followers of Christ.

I went to Israel and learned that God is *better* than I ever knew.

This understanding of who God is has changed me, and it's changing me still. I believe it will do the same for you. My time in Israel marked my life and shifted its direction entirely. I've been taking teams to Israel for biblical study trips ever since my first study trip in 2007. The gift given to me has become my gift to give others. My hope is for this study to be that gift to you.

The Bible was primarily written by Middle Easterners in a Middle Eastern context. Deeper insight into the Middle Eastern culture and historical context of the time in which the Bible was written will greatly add to our understanding of what the biblical authors meant by what they wrote and what the people described in the Bible did.

One of the major differences between Western and Eastern culture is *how* we teach and *how* we learn. We, in the West, are more of a Greco-Roman culture. We prize literature. We read sitting at desks, study with books in our hands, take notes, fill in the answers, and finish our workbooks.

Teaching and learning are different in the Middle East—they're different now, and they were different for Jesus in His time on earth. Middle Eastern teaching is visual; a rabbi teaches on the go. When Jesus taught, He could usually see the object of His lessons, and His disciples could see it too. This teaching style was not philosophical. It was right here. It was not "up there;" it was "down here."

Jesus' style wasn't to provide a syllabus or a workbook. He was more likely to walk through a field of mustard seed while sharing a parable about how the kingdom of God is like a mustard seed.

In the Middle Eastern tradition of learning, the student wants to stay very close to the rabbi so as not to lose any of his words. And the student never knows when or where the rabbi will begin teaching! In the Middle Eastern way, students learn through discovery rather than the acquisition of knowledge. This is how a rabbi teaches—he guides you into discovery. And this is how I want to guide you through our seven weeks together.

We are going to strive to view the Bible with a Middle Eastern lens and, at the same time, study a few Bible passages in a traditionally Jewish way, the way rabbis still teach the children in Israel today. We will walk into discoveries together rather than simply being taught the content or lesson.

This seven-week feast is my attempt to set a biblical table around which we can come together and discover Jesus' heart for women in His first-century world. At this table, we take off our Western lenses and put on our Middle Eastern lenses. I'll continue to share bits and pieces along the way to guide you in shaping your Middle Eastern lens.

I'm so honored and expectant to share in this seven-week biblical feast with you. In some ancient way, the Lord saw this for us before the foundations of the world were ever even laid. He's drawing us to this table, and *He* will do the feeding.

Posture yourself to receive.

All the best,

Kristi V. McLelland

HOW TO USE THIS STUDY

In our time together, we're going to study God's Word in a way that might seem a bit different from what you've experienced in the past. As I mentioned in the introduction, we are going to strive to view the Bible with a Middle Eastern lens and, at the same time, study a few Bible passages in a traditionally Jewish way, the way the rabbis would have taught Jesus the Bible, the way some rabbis still teach the children in Israel today.

With that in mind, let's discuss a bit of the framework for our study:

We approach the Scriptures as children expecting to be fed by our Father.
It can be easy to sit down with our Bibles and think something like, *OK, let me figure out some application from the passage I'm reading today.* I have good news for you—we are not spiritual orphans. We have a gracious heavenly Father who feeds us to the full with His Word; He gives abundantly. As we read the Word, we do our part by being open to what God will teach us. We posture ourselves to obey and to be gratefully fed by the Living God through His Word and by the power of His Spirit. But God is in charge of feeding us.

We're not looking for the "right" answer.
Though it may sound strange to our Western ears, in Judaism, the student with good questions is better than the student with all of the right answers. We never just read the Bible; we interact with it, asking questions of the text. We want to know what a text teaches us about God before we ask what it teaches us about ourselves. In our time together, we're going to focus on interacting with the biblical text in community, and we're going to learn to be OK with questions that cannot be easily answered and even questions that may leave us scratching our heads with a bit of mystery.

We want God's Word to become a part of who we are.
The Middle Eastern way of learning falls in line with more of an oral teaching tradition, less so the more formal learning style of our Western world. In our study together, we want these concepts in God's Word to get into our hearts and minds so much that they become a part of who we are, changing the way we see God and interact with the world. You'll notice we will revisit some of the same concepts each week; the study is intentionally crafted in this way. By the end of our time together, I hope these biblical concepts are so clear and familiar they are almost like second nature to you.

Learning will be a community endeavor in our time together.
In the Middle Eastern way, learning is very communal. Here's what I mean: in a Middle Eastern context, it would be common to see rabbis teaching students as they walk down the road. This teaching tradition places significant value on students discussing an issue with one another. Rabbis often instruct their students to "go first" and discuss what they believe about a teaching before the teacher explains the concept to them. We're going to adopt some of those ideas in our time together. In many cases, I'll "go first" in our feast teaching times. But you'll notice group discussion guides that I've crafted especially for you to use as you *yeshiva*, or discuss biblical texts together, after we begin unpacking them in our video teaching times.

Each week, you'll find the following sections:

The *Watch* section includes summaries of our video teaching, to help you as you follow along. Feel free to add your own notes here as you watch. You'll find detailed instructions on how to view the videos on the card inserted in the back of your Bible study book.

The *Discuss* section includes questions (based on the video teaching and the personal study each week) for your small group to explore together.

In the *Follow-up* section, we'll dive into further insight on a topic we discussed in our feast teaching times.

In the *Look* section, we'll highlight a Middle Eastern insight or cultural emphasis more in-depth to further your understanding of Jesus' first-century world.

In the *Learn* section, we'll take a passage of Scripture and consider it in light of a Middle Eastern lens.

In the *Live* section, we'll take some time to help you apply the concepts you're learning to your own life.

The *Watch* and *Discuss* times are meant to be completed with your small group. But the *Follow-up*, *Look*, *Learn*, and *Live* sections are for your personal study time. Instead of labeling them by days of study, we've labeled them by sections. Feel free to complete each between our weekly group times as you see fit throughout the week. Please note, terms in the text marked with this style are explained in further detail in the glossary on pages 144–153.

Let's get started.

MEETING THE MIDDLE EASTERN JESUS

As we prepare to watch our first video teaching together, we are getting ready to pull up our chairs for Session One of this biblical feast. I call our study times together feasts because we don't so much read the Word of God as *eat* it. We take it in—we let it do its work in us.

For me, the best meal is one I do not have to cook, and that's absolutely true when we come to the Word of God. God prepares this feast for us. We come to this moment and to this table believing the Living God will feed us. We are not orphans, and we are not fatherless. We do not have to scrounge, strive, or strain to feed ourselves the Word of God. We can simply, yet profoundly, posture ourselves to receive the feast the Lord has prepared for us—for you.

As we come to this biblical table, before you watch the video teaching, take a few moments to answer the following questions:

Why did you say yes to this feast?

What are you asking the Lord to do in your life through this seven-week feast?

Finish this sentence:

"I am here because my heart needs _____."

Sit back. Breathe deep. Enjoy the feast!

THE FEAST

Use the following notes and space provided during our feast teaching time. Feel free to add your own notes as you watch.

We eat the Word of God. It is sweeter than honey (Ps. 19:10).

We do not scrounge, strive, or strain to feed ourselves the Word of God. We posture ourselves to receive from God (Ps. 81:10).

We tend to stare at our lives and glance at God. We want to stare at God and glance at our lives.

The right hand in the biblical world was the hand of favor, honor, blessing, and sonship (Ps. 110:1).

We want to be a "right-hand people," who bless and honor others.

Western learning is different from Middle Eastern learning. Most of the Bible was written by Middle Easterners in a Middle Eastern context. In our time together, we want to learn to read the Bible through a Middle Eastern lens.

TO ACCESS THE VIDEO TEACHING SESSIONS, USE THE INSTRUCTIONS IN THE BACK OF YOUR BIBLE STUDY BOOK.

13

WESTERN LENS	MIDDLE EASTERN LENS
Form	Function
How? *How* did it happen?	Why? *Why* would God do that?
Understand ➔ Believe	Believe ➔ Understand
Law, Rule, Principle	Story, Narrative
What does it teach me about *me*?	What does it teach me about *God*?
Dig deep, get down in it … (Analysis—pick it apart)	Read through it … (Synthesis—bring it together)
Study to acquire *knowledge*	Posture to be *fed*

Reading the Bible through a Middle Eastern lens *adds* to our understanding of what the biblical authors and people featured in the Bible meant by what they *said* and *did*.

We want to live like rivers, not lakes. We want the Word to travel to us, through us, to others.

We have truly learned a thing when we can give it away.

LET'S YESHIVA!

As we discussed in our first "biblical feast" together, Middle Easterners most often learn and cultivate spiritual growth within the context of community and group conversation. With this cultural difference in mind, each week we're going to practice *yeshiva* together—what we might call "workshopping" or "brainstorming" around a topic in our Western culture—dialoguing openly about a biblical concept and walking together as a community with Jesus as our Rabbi. Discuss the following questions with your group.

What did you just *hear* or *see* in our feast together that you want to remember?

What one thing that we learned in our feast would you want to share with others this week?

What would it look like for you to posture yourself to receive when you read your Bible?

How does the concept of *eating* the Word of God differ from *reading* the Word of God?

Which element on the Western versus Middle Eastern Lens Chart (p. 14) stuck out to you the most?

What in your life right now makes you want to reach out and touch Jesus' wing?

What do you think people two thousand years ago would have noticed the most about Jesus?

What do you think would have made Jesus seem different or "other" to the people of His day?

YESHIVA

Today, *yeshiva* is a formal term referring to an established educational system that focuses on studying the Torah and the *Talmud*.[1]

In the first century, however, the emphasis lay in how a teacher interpreted a specific passage of Scripture or theological concept and whether that teaching was valid.[2] How would a community determine the validity of a biblical teaching? *Yeshiva.*

Stemming from the Hebrew verb meaning "to dwell," *yeshiva* occurred when students would discuss or debate questions or comments from a teacher.[3]

LIVING LIKE A RIVER, NOT A LAKE

I've been taking team members to the Jordan River for eleven years now. The Jordan River flows from the Sea of Galilee into the Dead Sea. The water moves, flows—it's living water, *mayim chayim*.[4] I've also floated in the Dead Sea for eleven years now. The water in the Dead Sea is still, motionless—it's dead water.

As a college professor, I tell my students all the time, "You haven't learned a thing when you've seen it. You haven't learned a thing when you've heard it. You haven't learned a thing when you have seen and heard it. You've learned a thing when you can give it away." We want the Word of God to travel through us to others, moving freely as a river would. We are not supposed to hold what God is teaching us to ourselves, motionless like the Dead Sea.

The things the Lord reveals to you—feeds you in this feast—are meant to travel through you to others. We want to live like rivers, not lakes.

Consider the following questions and record your answers below:
How can this feast travel through you this week?

Who needs to hear the truths you've learned at this week's feast?

Who can you be a river for this week?

TALLIT

The *tallit* is a prayer shawl. It has been used and is still used today in a variety of ways, depending on a person's tradition and orthodoxy. The *tallit* is often worn in prayer and worship.[6] In Numbers 15:37-40 and Deuteronomy 22:12, the Torah instructed the Israelites to put tassels (*tzitzit*) on the corners of their garments.[7]

TORAH

Just as Christians have subdivided the Old Testament into categories (for example, Law, History, Poetry, Major Prophets, Minor Prophets), the Jews have divided their sacred text. Torah is a section of Jewish Scripture that includes instruction and the Law.

For the Jews, nothing is more important than Torah. It's the first place they go when deriving authority from Scripture. The books of Torah include Genesis, Exodus, Leviticus, Numbers, and Deuteronomy—what scholars today call the Pentateuch (literally "five books"). Though traditionally translated as "law," the word *Torah* implies instruction more than law. According to Torah, the commandments offer freedom more than oppression. They serve as parameters that allow a person to function well in her family, tribe, and nation.[5]

The LORD said to Moses, "Speak to the Israelites and say to them: 'Throughout the generations to come you are to make tassels on the corners of your garments, with a blue cord on each tassel. You will have these tassels to look at and so you will remember all the commands of the LORD, that you may obey them and not prostitute yourselves by chasing after the lusts of your own hearts and eyes. Then you will remember to obey all my commands and will be consecrated to your God.'"
NUMBERS 15:37-40

Make tassels on the four corners of the cloak you wear.
DEUTERONOMY 22:12

Each *tzitzit* (tassel) contains several little knots—for a combined total of 613 knots on a *tallit*, each representing one of the commandments in the Torah.[8] Every time the Israelites saw the knots on the tassels, they were to remember the commandments. The Hebrew word used for the corner of the *tallit*, kanafayim (corners), can also mean "wings."[9] Likely, the tassels were permanently fixed on the corners or wings of the outer hem of the garment.

The Torah also instructed the Israelites to run a blue or violet cord through the tassels on their *tallits*. Both rabbinic sources and archaeological data tell us the blue dye used to color these tassels was made from a gland of the Murex snail (located in the Mediterranean). Each snail produced a very small amount of dye, making it very expensive.[10]

Each knot represents the commandments—the instructions to live in shalom—to keep the way of life in front of God's people.

Neighboring cultures used the colors blue and violet as symbols and signs for royalty. For the Israelites, this blue or violet cord may have been a sign or a symbol of the royal status of the entire community. The Israelite priests wore ephods, sleeveless garments, made with blue, purple, and scarlet yarn (Ex. 28:6). The blue cord in every Israelite's tassel symbolized they were *all* to be a royal priesthood among the nations—each and every one of them.

GOD NOT ONLY FREED THE ISRAELITES FROM SLAVERY, BUT HE IMMEDIATELY REMINDED THEM THAT HE MADE THEM REGAL AND ROYAL.

This idea of the royalty of the nation of Israel was tied to God's covenant relationship with them. The Israelites were not royal because of any worldly qualifications, but they were a royal community because they were God's people (Deut. 7:6-7). God set them apart with His love, and His love lifted them up.

God's choice to remind His people of their royal lineage in Him is especially impactful when you consider the fabric of Israelite culture and their national identity at the time God gave them this instruction. When God told them to run regal cords through their tassels, the people were still working to shed the national identity they had borne for so many years in Egypt, an identity associated with the onus of slavery. And God not only freed them from that slavery, but He immediately reminded them that He had made them regal and royal. It was as if God was saying, "I know what Egypt said you were and how you were mistreated there.

But I say you are a royal priesthood, a holy nation set apart by My love. Live in the identity I have given to you, forgetting any other label the world has tried to place on you."

READ MATTHEW 9:20-22.

In Matthew 9 we see a woman with an ongoing issue of blood that had lasted twelve years. This condition would have rendered her unclean according to Jewish law. Being considered unclean according to Jewish law had some significant effects on her day-to-day life. She would not have been able to attend temple or synagogue; in this time and culture, that prohibition amounted to effectively being cut off from the religious community and teaching. God's people and God's house, places where we often find refuge and solace today—especially in times of suffering—were not a refuge for her. In fact, the religious community had effectively turned its back on her and avoided association with her.

She would have been considered on the "outside" of the social world—in other words, "socially dead." These considerations are especially painful when you remember the communal nature of the Middle Eastern culture. This woman would have been shunned from society to the point that even her family members would not have been allowed to touch her or comfort her physically without becoming ceremonially unclean and excluded from the community until they could be ritually cleansed.[11] It's hard for us to fathom how alone she must have felt.

> Take a moment to imagine what this woman's world and life must have been like. What do you think she would have most desired? What do you think might have caused her the greatest pain?

This woman, the one who had been dealing with years of pain—physical, emotional, and spiritual—reached for the "edge" of Jesus' cloak (v. 20). The Greek word for "edge" used in this passage is *kraspedon*.[12] This same word appears in the Septuagint, the Greek translation of the Old Testament, in reference to the tassels that all Jews fixed on the "edges" or "corners/wings" of their outer garments. The Hebrew word for "edge" is *kanafayim*.

The woman with the issue of blood reached for Jesus' healing *kanafayim/kraspedon*—corner, edge, wing—of His *tallit*.

READ MALACHI 4:2.

Consider what it must have taken for this woman to reach out to Jesus—a woman who had been isolated from the community of God's people and access to spiritual teaching. I believe this woman acted out of significant faith. I think that in reaching out to grab the wing of Jesus' *tallit*, she was taking God at His Word in Malachi 4:2 and was asserting her belief in Jesus as the Son of God. In spite of all she had been through, in spite of the way the religious community had probably shunned her, she exerted faith in Jesus. She placed her hope in God's promises, in God's character.

This scene in Matthew 9 seems to be a literal fulfillment of Malachi 4:2—"the sun of righteousness will rise with healing in its wings" (CSB).

And don't miss this. In this moment, Jesus rewarded her faith, healed her, *and* brought her back to life within her Jewish community. He provided physical and spiritual healing. By reaching out to her, He helped usher her back into society and stuck up for her in the eyes of the world. In her cultural context, the idea of someone unclean touching a holy rabbi like Jesus would have been scandalous and risky. According to the tradition of the day, Jesus would have had every right to react harshly toward her and dismiss her, maybe even kill her. [13]

Pay close attention to Jesus' reaction here. He didn't condemn. He didn't dismiss. Instead, the Bible says Jesus turned to her, He saw her, and He said, "Take heart, daughter ... your faith has healed you" (Matt. 9:22). What a gospel-gorgeous truth. Praise the Living God.

> In what area of your life do you need to hear God say, "Take heart, daughter"? Describe it below. Feel free to use a journal if you need more room to write. How does this story from Matthew 9 encourage you in that circumstance?

CARRYING THE WILDERNESS WITH YOU

READ EXODUS 3:1-10.

 Look at this Bible passage through the **Western lens,** asking the question, "How did it happen?" Write down what you notice in this story.

 Look at this Bible passage through the **Middle Eastern lens,** asking the question, "Why would God do that?" Write down what you notice in this story.

This story happened in the desert, in the wilderness. Moses was tending his father-in-law's flock on "the far side of the wilderness" (v. 1). We often think of a desert or wilderness as something we want to get *out* of. But the Jewish people view the desert as the place where the Lord often meets His people and speaks to them.

The Lord met Moses in Exodus 3 in the desert and spoke to him. The Lord gave His Torah to His people at Mount Sinai in the desert (Ex. 20). He met Elijah in the desert and spoke to him in "a still small voice" (1 Kings 19:12, KJV). The Spirit led Jesus into the desert after His baptism. Angels attended to Him after His forty-day fast, His encounter with the devil, and His temptings (Matt. 4:1-11).

In the desert—the wilderness—God meets you and teaches you unique lessons that these dry and barren places frame in a way no other place would. In the Middle Eastern culture, the wilderness is seen almost as a sacred place, a place of intimacy, where God speaks a "word" (*davar*) to you. [14]

This story of Moses in the desert is about the Living God who "[saw] the misery of [His] people in Egypt" (Ex. 3:7a). He "heard them crying out because of their slave drivers" (v. 7b). He was "concerned about their suffering" (v. 7b). He responded to what He saw and heard by coming down to rescue them. In the Bible, when we read that the Lord "sees" or "hears" something, those words signal to us that He is going to *act*. (It's not as if God has missed something—as if He were a man who could turn away and miss a glimpse or whisper of something that has happened. God is omnipresent; He sees and hears everything that happens to us.) He is responsive, alive, awake—ever-ready to come to the rescue, to attend to His children in guidance and love.

This story isn't so much about a burning bush but about the Living God who refuses to look away. He chooses to see, to hear, to let it matter—to let it all matter. And it's about the Living God who isn't afraid to come down, get in the middle of the ruins of this world, and put His hands all over them to restore us. We run from drama. The Lord runs into it to bring rescue, restoration, and renewal.

When we are in a desert or wilderness season of life, we often ask, "How long do I have to be in this wilderness or desert?" Or we ask, "How do I get out of this difficult wilderness season?" But in the Middle East, they ask the questions, "How do I carry the wilderness with me?" "How do I remember the word the Lord taught me in the wilderness?"

Are you more likely to fear wilderness seasons and try to get out of them as quickly as possible? Or do you usually see them as a time of growth and intimacy with God, despite the difficulty? Explain.

THE LIVING GOD ISN'T AFRAID TO COME DOWN, GET IN THE MIDDLE OF THE RUINS OF THIS WORLD, AND PUT HIS HANDS ALL OVER THEM TO RESTORE US.

What would need to change in your heart for you to trust God more fully in wilderness seasons?

Who do you know who's going through a wilderness season right now?

How can you encourage him or her to listen for God in the desert?

LIVING FORWARD

Therefore I am now going to allure her;
I will lead her into the wilderness
and speak tenderly to her.
There I will give her back her vineyards,
and will make the Valley of Achor a door of hope.
There she will respond as in the days of her youth,
as in the day she came up out of Egypt.
"In that day," declares the LORD,
"you will call me 'my husband';
you will no longer call me 'my master.'
I will betroth you to me forever;
I will betroth you in righteousness and justice,
in love and compassion.
I will betroth you in faithfulness,
and you will acknowledge the LORD."
HOSEA 2:14-16,19-20

You may be familiar with the message of the Book of Hosea. The prophet Hosea (under the inspiration of the Holy Spirit) compared God's relationship with His people to a marriage relationship—a marriage in which Israel, God's people, was repeatedly unfaithful to God.

In the Hosea 2 passage above, we find an almost shocking illustration of God's covenant faithfulness to His children. The Living God marries His people in the wilderness, the desert, despite their unfaithfulness to the covenant He made with them. This passage pictures God's extraordinary, sacrificial love.

Israel would go on to do her worst while God did His best. She would chase after the gods of the nations. In other words, the bride in this illustration, the people of Israel, would not live up to her marriage vows. She would prostitute herself before the nations—just as Gomer was unfaithful in her marriage to Hosea (3:1). But God's love runs longer than our sin, and His atonement covers the whole of our sin. God and God alone would keep the marriage covenant. The Lord married Israel knowing she would not be able to keep every law, every commandment, and every vow. He did it because He knew He could and would. He knew that the Lamb of God would come one day to take away every sin.

The Lord drew Israel into the desert and spoke to her there. The place that seemed to only represent barrenness became one of restoration and redemption, of covenant pledge, of love everlasting. To me, Hosea 2 is one of the most beautiful passages in the whole Bible. It is so intimate, so intentional—the covenant love and promise of the Lord given to His people *in* the desert.

The Lord often speaks to His people in a special way in wilderness seasons. We want to carry these lessons and these times of intimate fellowship from the wilderness with us as we live and walk forward.

When was the last time you were in a desert or wilderness season? Describe the situation below.

What did you learn during that time?

How did you see God respond on your behalf in that wilderness season?

How can the things learned in that wilderness season travel forward with you and strengthen you as you live your life?

How can you keep the lessons of the wilderness with you instead of dismissing them or trying to forget them?

SESSION TWO

JESUS AND WOMAN IN THE FIRST-CENTURY WORLD

This week, we are going to look at two things present in every interaction Jesus had with a woman in the New Testament Gospels. In each story, Jesus brought two things into the woman's life. We will learn to look for these two things in His interactions with the feminine in the first-century world.

We will also sketch a brief history of woman within Israel, starting in Genesis and heading into the Gospel-era of the New Testament. Woman had a good beginning, a good genesis. God created woman with dignity and honor, and the culture of early civilization recognized the *imago dei* in her. Her presence, contribution, and leadership showed up in culture all over the world again and again.

However, Jesus was born into a world where woman had lost her honorable standing in society's eyes. In our teaching time together this week, we will sketch a history of how this cultural shift may have happened. More importantly, we will begin to see how Jesus came into the world to lift woman out of her shame and restore her honor.

Before you watch the teaching video, take a few moments to answer the following questions.

As we come to this biblical table:
What have you been thinking about since last week's feast?

Who did you live like a river toward last week and share what you learned at the feast?

How did that conversation go? How did your time together challenge you or confirm what you've been learning?

As we pull up our chairs for Session Two of this biblical feast, we are again posturing ourselves to receive—to be fed the Word of God by the Lord Himself. In some ancient way, He has set this table for us, and He is the One who has drawn us to it. He wants to meet us *in* this feast, at the table He is preparing for us. Remember, we want to stare at the Lord and glance at our lives.

Sit back. Breathe deep. Enjoy the feast!

THE FEAST

Use the following notes and space provided during our feast teaching time. Feel free to add your own notes as you listen.

Remember, Middle Easterners primarily wrote the Bible in a Middle Eastern context.

Every culture has idioms—sayings, phrases—that are widely understood among its people.

The Bible has *Jewish idioms*—sayings, phrases—that Jewish people would have readily known and understood.

WESTERN LENS	MIDDLE EASTERN LENS
Form	Function
How? *How* did it happen?	Why? *Why* would God do that?
Understand ➔ Believe	Believe ➔ Understand
Law, Rule, Principle	Story, Narrative
What does it teach me about *me*?	What does it teach me about *God*?
Dig deep, get down in it ... (Analysis—pick it apart)	Read through it ... (Synthesis—bring it together)
Study to acquire *knowledge*	Posture to be *fed*

As a Western culture, we are more Athens and Rome than we are Jerusalem. We are more Greco-Roman than we are Semitic or Jewish. Consequently, we tend to want to understand before we believe. But the Middle Eastern way is to believe God, to take Him at His Word, with the idea that understanding will come out of our belief.

Woman had a very good beginning within Israel's history. Women like Eve, Miriam, Deborah, Jael, Abigail, Esther, and Ruth were held in honor and given respect.

Through influential teachings and teachers during the Intertestamental Period, women lost much of their social standing. Instead of being held in honor, women were denigrated to a place of shame.

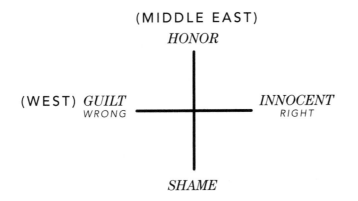

Pious, virtuous Jewish men who stood up against the invasion of Hellenism and "Vegas" took it too far.

Jesus was born into a world where Ben Sira theology had been spreading and growing for approximately two hundred years.[1]

Jesus brought *justice* and *righteousness* to women in the first-century world. He generously lifted them up out of their shame and restored their honor.

Jesus did not come to turn things upside down. Jesus came to turn things right side up.

LET'S YESHIVA!

Each week we're going to take some time to *yeshiva*—to emulate the Middle Eastern communal way of discussing spiritual concepts and growing together in grace as a biblical community. Discuss the following questions with your group.

What did you just *hear* or *see* in our feast together that you want to remember?

What one thing that we learned in our feast would you want to share with others this week?

Have you found yourself staring at the Lord more this week and glancing at your life? Or vice versa? Explain.

If you find yourself staring at your life and glancing at the Lord, what one thing could you do differently this week to help shift your gaze?

How has Jesus brought *mishpat* (justice) and *tzedakah* (righteousness) into your life?

Can you share a story or tell of a time when God generously lifted you up?

In the Middle East, to have a *good eye* means you are generous.[2] Who is the most generous person you know? Why do you consider him or her to be generous? Do you have a *good eye*?

What did you think of the brief sketch of the history of woman in Israel? Was anything surprising?

What stuck out to you from our feast this week?

MISHPAT

Translated most often as "justice," the Hebrew word *mishpat* serves a special function in the economy of God. Since God advocates for the poor and the oppressed, especially widows and orphans, He expects His followers to do the same. At its core, *mishpat* isn't so much a question of innocence and guilt as much as honor and shame. To bring justice to the world, God exalts the humble by raising them to honor and covering their shame.

Tied closely to the word *tzedakah*, or "righteousness," *mishpat* deals with punishment for wrongdoing, but it is also concerned about equal rights for all—rich and poor, female and male, foreigner and native-born.[3]

ABUNDANT LIFE

"Scripture is like a river ... broad and deep; shallow
enough here for the lamb to go wading but deep
enough there for the elephant to swim."[4]
—Gregory The Great

The Bible is living and active and so are we. When we sit down
with our Bibles, it is life with life—the life that God has placed
in us through His Holy Spirit interacting with the living Word
of God. When the living Word of God collides with the life
of God inside of us it generates more life—it leads to what
the Jews call *L'chaim*—a phrase that literally means "to life!"[5]
A flourishing. An abundance. A buoyancy.

Refining that comes in time spent with God acts as a
calibration, helping us understand how God created life to be.
He brings the best of life to us. And, though the world and its
circumstances occupy so much of our time and emotional energy,
the Bible gives us a glimpse into actual reality. The Bible shows
us what is really true about God, about us, and about the world
around us. We take it in; we let it do its work.

When it comes to your relationship with the Bible,
do you feel more like a lamb or an elephant? Why?

Do you believe that God's Word and ways bring you
abundant life? Do you believe it intellectually and in
the way you live? Explain.

TZEDAKAH

Tzedakah means
"righteousness" and so
much more. Placed within
the realm of relationships,
tzedakah prompts us to
make things right through
generosity.

Another translation for
this word could easily
be "mercy." In fact, in the
first-century world, giving
to the poor was seen as an
act of righteousness.
(See Matt. 6:1-4.)

By not sharing generously,
one violates the very
justice, will, and command
of God. *Tzedakah* is
not optional in God's
economy.[6]

The eastern set of Huldah Gates as they stand today

HULDAH

BEIT

Beit is the Hebrew word for "house."

In Jesus' first-century world, hospitality and communal living were central to the culture. So it comes as no surprise that the ideas of house and affiliation were also very important. You were not so much known for your job or your work, but for your people and the house you were part of.

Solomon built the Lord a temple—or a *beit* (house). The temple in Jerusalem was the Lord's house. He lived in Jerusalem with and among His people.[7]

We have one more addition to the list of godly Israelite women in the Old Testament that we discussed in our feast this week—Huldah, a prophetess during the reign of King Josiah. Second Kings 22–23 and 2 Chronicles 34 tell her story.

READ 2 KINGS 22–23.

From this story, we come to understand that the Torah, the Law that told God's people how to please Him and governed the nation of Israel, had been lost for some time. When the long-lost Torah was discovered in the temple by Hilkiah, the high priest, it was brought to King Josiah. Shaphan, the secretary, read it aloud to Josiah. After hearing it, Josiah tore his robes, a sign of grief and mourning in the Hebrew culture (2 Kings 22:11). Josiah realized how deeply Israel had strayed from the way of the Lord as prescribed in the Law. He saw firsthand how far Israel had fallen in terms of obedience to the Lord God. King Josiah ruled a nation in need of deep repentance, change, reform, and revival.

What should he do? With the nation on the line, to which of God's prophets would Josiah reach out for counsel? King Josiah had several prophets at his disposal—Jeremiah, Zephaniah, Nahum, Habakkuk, and Huldah. I imagine the names of the first four prophets just mentioned are familiar to you—each of these men penned books through the inspiration of the Holy Spirit that are now part of Israel's collection of prophets (our Old Testament) and named after them.

It might seem like the logical choice to consult one of those men—it's clear God used them mightily in their time. But with this wealth of wise prophets to choose from, King Josiah consulted Huldah. She prophesied that disaster would fall upon Jerusalem and the kingdom of Judah. She also prophesied that Josiah would not see this calamity in his lifetime because his heart had been responsive and humble before the Lord. Both of these prophecies came to pass.

> HULDAH WAS CREDITED WITH HELPING TURN THE NATION OF ISRAEL BACK TO GOD AND CONSEQUENTLY SPARING A GENERATION OF GOD'S PEOPLE.

Huldah became a well-known figure in Israel's history for her role in Josiah's reforms. In concert with Josiah, Huldah was credited with helping turn the nation of Israel back to God and consequently sparing a generation of God's people from His wrath and judgment. Years later when Herod's temple was built in Jerusalem (expanding Zerubbabel's temple), the gates where pilgrims and worshipers entered and exited the temple were named the Huldah Gates. Huldah's name was known by all who came to Jerusalem to worship the Living God at His *beit* (house).

The two Huldah Gates on the south were used both for entrance and exit.[8]
MISHNAH MIDDOT 1:3

It is incredible to think that the very gates by which people entered the temple of God were named after a woman. What an honor!

When I take teams to Israel, we sit in front of the Huldah Gates on the Southern Rabbinic Teaching Steps leading up to the southern wall of the Temple Mount for one of our biblical classes. For hundreds

MISHNAH

When God gave His Torah to Moses at Mount Sinai, Jews believe He also gave a second set of laws called *Mishnah* or "that which is repeated."[9] According to this line of thinking, the written Torah (or *Mikra*) was far greater in importance, but the oral Torah (or *Mishnah*) expanded and explained the meaning of the written Torah.

By the beginning of the third century AD, a man known as Yehudah ha-Nasi, or in English, Judah the Prince, led a project to record the traditions that had been handed down to that point.[10]

This written document offers a small window into Judaism from 300 BC to approximately AD 200.[11] It is divided into six main sections, with those subdivided into seven to twelve subsections, starting with the longest and ending with the shortest.[12]

of years, pilgrims would come to Jerusalem in observance of the three foot festivals given in Deuteronomy 16—Passover, Pentecost (the Feast of Weeks), and the Feast of Tabernacles. (In the Middle Eastern culture, many things are named or labeled literally. These were called "foot festivals" because the people traveled by foot three times a year to attend them.)

As the worshipers ascended the Southern Steps to enter the temple through the Huldah Gates, they may have sung the psalms of ascent (Pss. 120–134), psalms of praise written for the pilgrimage to the temple.[13] These psalms are rhythmic and melodic. Worshipers during that time didn't read the psalms the way we do; they sang them. Imagine traveling to Jerusalem from far away. You've finally reached the city after a long journey, and as you walk up the steps to enter God's house (temple), you sing the following:

> I lift up my eyes to the mountains—
> where does my help come from?
> My help comes from the LORD
> the Maker of heaven and earth.
> He will not let your foot slip—
> he who watches over you will not slumber;
> indeed, he who watches over Israel
> will neither slumber nor sleep.
> The LORD watches over you—
> the LORD is your shade at your right hand;
> the sun will not harm you by day,
> nor the moon by night.
> The LORD will keep you from all harm—
> he will watch over your life;
> the LORD will watch over your coming and going
> both now and forevermore.
> **PSALM 121**

It would have been such a celebratory moment, seeing the house of God—where your help comes from—with the long pilgrimage over, ready to finally be in the presence of the one true God. I imagine worshipers experienced levity, laughter, and joy upon arriving at the Lord's house to worship Him with their Israelite brothers and sisters.

MANNA

READ EXODUS 16:1-5,13-17,31-36.

Look at this Bible passage through the **Western lens**, the framework of understanding first and allowing that understanding to fuel belief. Write down what you notice in this story.

The children of Israel complained + said they wished they had not been taken from Egypt.

Look at this Bible passage through the **Middle Eastern lens**, the framework of believing first and allowing that belief to fuel understanding. Write down what you notice in this story.

God provided exactly what they needed. They never went hungry.

In this beautiful story, we see a moment when the Israelites believed God and understanding followed.

The Book of Exodus tells the story of the Hebrews' liberation from Egyptian tyranny and slavery. After around 430 years of slavery and forced labor in Egypt, the Lord miraculously delivered them out of Egypt, through the Red Sea.[14] Those years of slavery changed them. When they crossed the Red Sea to their freedom, they were a haggard, emaciated, disoriented, and confused people. With Egypt behind them and the desert in front of them, the Israelites walked into an unknown future with God.

The people of God, freshly liberated from slavery, had no idea how to live free after something like 430 years of bondage. They were in the desert, and they were hungry. One morning they woke up, walked out of their tents, looked down on the ground, and saw something—something they had never seen before.

> When the Israelites saw it, they said to each other, "What is it?"
> For they did not know what it was.
> **EXODUS 16:15**

In Exodus 16 we read an account of when the Lord began providing manna for His people. The Bible calls it "bread from heaven" (Ex. 16:4). Manna was also described as "white like coriander seed and [tasting] like wafers made with honey" (v. 31).

The Hebrew word for manna is manhue (or ha-man depending on the transliteration you use)—and the sense of the word comes in the form of a question. *Manhue* means, "What is it?"[15] The Israelites were hungry. They ate the manna without knowing what it was. They ate a mystery because they knew it came from the hand of God. They trusted the source and bit down on the unknown—literally.

They ate the "What is it?" and found out exactly what it was—God's faithful provision for them in the desert for what, unbeknownst to them, would be forty years. He provided manna every day except for the Sabbath. The Israelites were told to gather two days worth of food on the day preceding Sabbath. The Lord never failed them. He never skipped a day. He never went on vacation and forgot about them. Most important of all, He never ran out. God's people learned that His provision is inexhaustible; He continues to give and give. He is trustworthy. You can afford to believe Him, to take Him at His word, and *then* walk into understanding.

HE IS TRUSTWORTHY. YOU CAN AFFORD TO BELIEVE HIM, TO TAKE HIM AT HIS WORD, AND *THEN* WALK INTO UNDERSTANDING.

Is there a difficult situation, circumstance, or relationship in your life right now, one it's hard to believe God could ever change? Describe it below.

Can you recount, remember, or retell the story of a time in your life when God met you in a struggle or provided for you? Describe it below.

How can that past story of struggle and remembering God's provision encourage you in the difficult situation you're currently facing?

The Israelites ate manna forty years, until they came to a land that was settled; they ate manna until they reached the border of Canaan.
EXODUS 16:35

On the evening of the fourteenth day of the month, while camped at Gilgal on the plains of Jericho, the Israelites celebrated the Passover. The day after the Passover, that very day, they ate some of the produce of the land: unleavened bread and roasted grain. The manna stopped the day after they ate this food from the land; there was no longer any manna for the Israelites, but that year they ate of the produce of Canaan.
JOSHUA 5:10-12

God's provision for His children was so precise that He stopped sending manna the day after the Israelites ate the fruit of the land of Canaan. His promised provision carried them to the promised land. Like the Israelites, we are living on the Lord's promises to us, and He will not let us down.

But He doesn't promise to tell us everything that's going on ahead of time. He doesn't promise we'll see a blueprint before we start building. The reward is often on the other side of obedience. The Levites stepped into the Jordan River with the ark of the covenant and *then* the waters split (Josh. 3). Life doesn't always afford us all the facts before we make a decision. But we can always decide to trust God's character. We can always decide to believe in God's goodness and steadfast love.

THE REWARD IS OFTEN ON THE OTHER SIDE OF OBEDIENCE.

Eating a mystery requires faith in the God providing the mystery. If we wait until we understand it all, we will never move, never set out, never know what could have been. Waiting until we understand the situation can render us paralyzed of heart—too afraid to lean into the new and next things because they are unknown.

We look into the mystery and say, "What is it?" When you know it's the Lord leading, prompting, speaking, moving—eat the mystery. Lean into it and see where it takes you. Lean into the mystery and watch the Living God provide.

In what situation, circumstance, or relationship in your life right now do you think God might be asking you to believe Him and trust Him before you fully understand? Describe it below.

What, if anything, is keeping you from trusting God with this situation, circumstance, or relationship? Explain.

Do you believe the reward is often on the other side of obedience? Why or why not?

EATING A MYSTERY

The Israelites ate manna in the desert for forty years until they entered Canaan. *Manhue* is a question—"What is it?" In the desert, the Israelites ate a mystery, something they did not know or understand, because they knew it came from the Lord. Sometimes in His provision for us, the Lord asks us to trust Him and move forward without having all the answers, to trust He will sustain us even in the things that feel like a mystery to us. We tend to be a people who want certainty, clarity, surety, and full understanding *before* we move, but God doesn't promise to provide those answers every time.

Can you think of a time when you "ate the mystery" because you knew it was the Lord leading you, prompting you, guiding you into something unknown?

When was the last time you said yes to something without having all the facts first?

How did it turn out? Are you still in the midst of it?

Call, text, or email a friend this week and ask her to share a story of a time when she "ate a mystery" too. Sharing our stories of God's provision brings Him glory, and it serves to fuel our future faith.

SESSION THREE

JESUS AND THE WOMAN AT THE WELL

Jesus was born into a world where Ben Sira's ideology and theology of women had traveled and grown for approximately two hundred years.[1] He was born into a world where woman was not held in honor in the culture. She was instead shrouded in shame. Jesus brought *mishpat* (justice) and *tzedakah* (righteousness) to women. He brought a generous lifting up to women in His first-century world.

This week we will eat our first biblical story of Jesus' interaction with a woman. As you take part in our feast, and in the future when you read stories of Jesus and women, continue to look for how Jesus brings justice and righteousness—a generous lifting up.

We take heart as daughters. If Jesus did it for her, He can certainly do it for us.

As we come to this biblical table:
What have you been thinking about since last week's feast?

God cares about every aspect of our lives & He provides for every need.

Justice & Righteousness

Who did you live like a river toward last week and share what you learned at the feast?

How did that conversation go? How did your time together challenge you or confirm what you've been learning?

We are getting ready to pull up our chairs for Session Three of this biblical feast. More than reading the Word of God, we seek to eat it. We want to take it in and let it do its work. We approach the Word as daughters—we lean back, look up, open wide our mouths, and trust God will feed us. We posture ourselves to receive.

Sit back. Breathe deep. Enjoy the feast!

THE FEAST

Use the following notes and space provided during our feast teaching time. Feel free to add your own notes as you watch.

Jesus entered the first-century world and practiced both compassion and empathy. He showed both toward the women with whom He interacted in His life and ministry.

COMPASSION
cum = with[2]

pathos = pain[4]

EMPATHY
em = in[3]

pathos = pain

He was not afraid to sit with women who were in pain. He was not afraid to enter into their pain with them.

One overarching statement precedes the seven "I Am" statements in the Gospel of John. The seven "I Am" statements hang on this one statement. In other words, the seven "I Am" statements can be true because this first statement is true.

WESTERN LENS	MIDDLE EASTERN LENS
Form	Function
How? *How* did it happen?	Why? *Why* would God do that?
Understand ➜ Believe	Believe ➜ Understand
Law, Rule, Principle	Story, Narrative
What does it teach me about *me*?	What does it teach me about *God*?
Dig deep, get down in it … (Analysis—pick it apart)	Read through it … (Synthesis—bring it together)
Study to acquire *knowledge*	Posture to be *fed*

#4

There are two kinds of water in the Middle East: dead water and living water. Dead water is still water; like water in a cistern, it doesn't move. Living water is moving water, like water in wells, rivers, and streams. In the first-century world, people preferred to be baptized in living water.[5]

The Jewish/Samaritan schism was approximately seven hundred years old when Jesus came on the scene. Jews and Samaritans worshiped at two separate temples and used different canons of Scripture.

The Middle East, both then and now, has three primary cultural norms:

□ Honor/Shame
□ Hospitality
□ Communal living (we, not me)[6]

Jews living in Galilee sometimes traveled through Samaria to get to Judea. Historically, this route was difficult to traverse since Jews and Samaritans were at odds; however, we see it became an opportunity for Jesus to bring *mishpat* and *tzedakah* to a Samaritan woman.

Jesus named her shame, not her sin. He named her pain and sat with her in it. He started generously lifting her up. He sat at a well and waited for her. He reached out to her and spoke first—He bridged the gap. He asked if He could drink after her, treating her as clean, not unclean. He started talking about living water with her while sitting at a well, a source of living water. He respected her by talking theology of worship with her. She was the first person whom He told He was the Messiah. She became the missionary—a witness—to her community.

The Samaritan woman will forever hold the honor of being the first person Jesus explicitly told He was the Messiah, the Christ.

WHY TRAVEL THROUGH SAMARIA?

In John 4:4 we read that Jesus "had to go through Samaria."

History tells us many Galilean Jews avoided Samaria altogether on their way to Jerusalem, even traveling longer and going out of their way to circumvent the region where Samaritans lived.[7]

So what might be going on in this John 4 passage?

Why might Jesus have "had to go through Samaria"?

I think Jesus *chose* to go through Samaria because He wanted to bring restoration to that deep and ancient seven-hundred-year-old schism between the Jews and Samaritans.

After the moment in John 4 with Jesus and the Samaritan woman at the well, we might imagine Him and His disciples stopping and staying in ancient Sychar when they would pass through the area. Perhaps Jesus and His disciples became really good friends with this woman and the Samaritans in her village. Perhaps Jesus brought peace to ancient Sychar through His interaction with this woman.

La Heim –
Justice + Righteousness were a part
of every interaction Jesus had
with women.

The verse before the "7" I AM statements
John 4

Psalms 1:   meditate = Hagah   ~~Hebrew means to~~ devour

Israelites + Samarians had a disagreement
for more than 700 years.

Half Jewish/Half Assyrian = Samaritan

Assyria attacked northern Israel.

Mishpat = justice   tzedakah = righteousness

The spit of a Samaritan woman is unclean.

Woman at the well is without friends = alone.

Jesus asks for a drink from her cup which
was considered unclean.

Matt 19:1-3 Jesus talks about legality of
divorce for burning the bread.

Jesus names her shame in that she was divorced
      5 times, left in shame,

Israel is an honor/shame culture
and a hospitality culture -
Hebrew
Haver = friend
John 4:24 - rabbi is speaking theology with a
Samaritan woman at noon where everyone
could see them.
Jesus said - I am the one speaking to you
am the Messiah. "I AM" statements follow.
John 4:39 - they believed the testimony of the
woman + He stayed and preached to them.
Many Samaritans were saved.

Cara Murphy -

LET'S YESHIVA!

Each week we're going to take some time to *yeshiva*—to emulate the Middle Eastern communal way of discussing spiritual concepts and growing together in grace as a biblical community. Discuss the following questions with your group.

What did you just *hear* or *see* in our feast together that you want to remember?
Jesus reached out to her at her level

What one thing that we learned in our feast would you want to share with others this week? *You can come to Him now.*

How has Jesus brought *mishpat* (justice) and *tzedakah* (righteousness) into your life this week?

In this season of life, does your heart feel more like "dead water" or "living water"? Explain.

Who are your *haverim*? Who helps you carry your water?

HAVER (PL. HAVERIM)

A Hebrew word literally meaning "friend" or "companion." In the first-century world, a haver was a study partner and fellow disciple—someone you could ask hard questions of and someone who you could expect to ask you hard questions in return.

Haverim pushed each other, sometimes to the brink, in order to get to the truth. If you called someone your *haver* in the first-century world, it also implied that you followed the Torah in a similar fashion. You might even follow the same rabbi.

You might spend the majority of your days with these *haverim* discussing the most important issues in your life and the lives of those around you.[8]

DEVOURING GOD'S WORD

But their delight is in the law of the LORD, and on his law they meditate day and night.
PSALM 1:2 (NRSV)

When you think of meditating on a passage of Scripture, what imagery or actions come to mind?

Mull it over — Look at it from various angles → think about it → chew on it.

I'm not sure what you wrote in your answer above. But when I think of "meditating" in our cultural context today, I usually think of something quiet that includes pondering an idea or spiritual truth, an activity I might do alone. But that's not what the original audience of the Bible would have had in mind when they read Psalm 1:2. This is a great example of how we tend to interpret biblical words and concepts in current meaning and imagery common to us today.

This word "meditate" in the original Hebrew language is *hagah*.[9] It means to eat or devour something, like a lion eats its prey.[10] The sense of the word is fierce and active.

Jesus was born into a culture with an oral communication tradition. Rabbis memorized the Old Testament texts and taught the Scriptures from memory. Spiritual growth was often in the context of community. Spiritual leaders taught the Scriptures orally. Those in spiritual community with one another would then dialogue about what a Bible passage meant, in a sense wrestling with God's Word as a community of faith. Their community of faith and communal contending with God's Word fed their personal faith and devotion. In this line of thinking, followers of God grapple with His Word to understand who He is in order to walk His path of life, to live in a way that pleases God, obeying Him, and flourishing under His care. "*Hagah-ing*" a passage led to obedience, walking the path of life with God.

FOLLOWERS OF GOD GRAPPLE WITH HIS WORD TO UNDERSTAND WHO HE IS IN ORDER TO LIVE IN A WAY THAT PLEASES GOD, FLOURISHING UNDER HIS CARE.

Men "hagah-ing" a passage of Scripture.

In some ways, our Western understanding of meditating on God's Word is similar to the context of the original Hebrew. When we *hagah* a passage, we take it in, and it becomes a part of who we are. It fuels our devotion to God. In the first century, Jews would describe a spiritual truth that they meditated on as "becoming a part of their fabric"—in other words, becoming a part of who they are. When we turn a spiritual truth over and over in our hearts and minds, it becomes a part of who we are; it becomes "a part of our fabric." And with those new truths inside of us, we have the ability to know God more fully and walk the path of life with Him.

We can *hagah,* or meditate on, a passage alone, but eating is much better together. We want to devour the Word of God like a lion eating its prey.

Consider the following questions:
What would it look like for you to *hagah* in your spiritual community?

Studying with a "family" of believers

What biblical truths have become a part of the fabric of who you are recently?

God loves it when we praise Him!

How have those truths fueled your faith?

JACOB'S WELL

> Jacob's well was there, and Jesus, tired as he was from the journey, sat down by the well. It was about noon.
> **JOHN 4:6**

When the Lord introduced Himself to Moses in Exodus 3, He introduced Himself by saying, "I am the God of your father, the God of Abraham, the God of Isaac and the God of Jacob" (Ex. 3:6). Jacob was one of the patriarchal fathers of the Jewish people. Jacob's well was dug in the days of Genesis.

Hundreds and hundreds of years later, Jesus sat with the Samaritan woman at this very well. In Jesus' day, the well was located in a city called Sychar, at the base of Mount Gerizim—the mountain the Samaritan woman mentioned, the one where the Samaritans worshiped.[14] The Samaritans had built a temple on the top of Mount Gerizim because they were not permitted to worship at the temple in Jerusalem.[15]

Jacob's well still exists today—some nearly two thousand years after Jesus sat at it with the Samaritan woman. The name of the city where it's located has changed; it's now called Nablus. The well is still located at the base of Mount Gerizim. To this very day, Samaritans still live on Mount Gerizim, and you can see the ruins and remains of the Samaritan temple toward the top of the mountain.

Jacob's well is one of my favorite sites. I love taking teams to Jacob's well when we are in the Holy Land. While we're there, I invite the women to circle around the well and read the entire story of John 4 out loud, one verse at a time.

I love giving women that special moment—reading the story of the woman at the very well where the story took place some two thousand years earlier.

MOUNT GERIZIM

Second in height in the Nablus region only to its neighbor Mount Ebal, *Mount Gerizim* serves as the most sacred location for Samaritans.[11]

In approximately 128 BC, Jews destroyed the Samaritan temple and attempted forced conversion on all the people groups living in the land, including the Samaritans. Needless to say, this attack enlivened the Samaritans, and animosity between the Jews and the Samaritans piqued in the first centuries BC and AD.[12]

Mount Gerizim overshadows what was the city of Sychar in the New Testament, specifically Jacob's well. Because of its proximity, the site figures prominently in the conversations Jesus has with the Samaritan woman in John 4.[13]

Mount Gerizim

JESUS REALLY CAME TO EARTH TO SET THINGS RIGHT. THE BIBLE SHOWS US HOW GOD DESIGNED THE WORLD TO WORK, HOW HE MADE OUR HEARTS, AND HOW LIFE REALLY IS.

After reading the story in John 4, the women then take turns winding the crank and bringing water up from Jacob's well in a tin pail. The well still produces water—cool and clear.

In a similar way, this story still moves us, speaks to us, and travels through us as we share it with others. The Bible isn't just the best story ever told—it is also the truest. These stories really happened. Jesus really came to earth to set things right. The Bible shows us how God designed the world to work, how He made our hearts, and how life really is.

Jacob's well as it appears today

HILLEL VS. SHAMMAI

READ MATTHEW 19:1-9.

Look at this Bible passage through the **Western lens**, identifying the law, rule, or principle at hand. Write down what you notice in this story.

Once a couple is married, divorce is not an option except for sexual immorality.

Look at this Bible passage through the **Middle Eastern lens**, identifying it as part of the biblical story or narrative. Write down what you notice in this story.

From the very beginning God created man and woman to be joined become one flesh. Let no man separate them.

One generation before Jesus, there were two main religious houses or schools in Jerusalem. Both schools were very influential throughout Judaism and maintained incredibly influential leaders as their heads.

One school followed *Rabbi Hillel*[16] and the other *Rabbi Shammai*.[17] Hillel's grandson was named Gamaliel. You may recognize his name; he was the rabbi that the apostle Paul studied under (Acts 22:3).

Hillel was a "spirit of the Law" kind of guy. Shammai, on the other hand, was a "letter of the Law" kind of guy. Hillel and Shammai often read the same Scripture and came up with different interpretations and methods of application. Hillel was usually wider in his interpretations, meaning he typically gave more grace and leeway where the Law was more open to interpretation. Shammai was usually much more narrow in his interpretations, meaning he was typically more rigid and conservative when the Law proved somewhat ambiguous.[18]

During Hillel and Shammai's day there was a widespread debate over the interpretation of Deuteronomy 24:1. It was one of the hot topics in their generation.[19]

> "If a man marries a woman who becomes displeasing to him because he finds something indecent about her, and he writes her a certificate of divorce, gives it to her and sends her from his house."
> **DEUTERONOMY 24:1**

The debate of the day centered on what the word *indecent* meant in this Deuteronomy text in the Torah. Whatever *indecent* meant, it was grounds for a man to divorce his wife and send her away.

According to Rabbi Hillel, *indecent* could be many things. In Hillel's view, a man could divorce his wife for something as simple as burning the bread, among many other things.[20]

Rabbi Shammai taught a very different interpretation of the word *indecent*. For Shammai, the only indecent thing that provided grounds for a man to divorce his wife was adultery.[21]

In Jesus' world, men alone had the power to divorce their wives; a woman could not initiate divorce proceedings against her husband. This cultural practice created a gender inequity in marriage and left women vulnerable to mistreatment and easy abandonment.

"The right to divorce was exclusively the husband's."[22]
—J. JEREMIAS

"In this way the Hillelite view made the unilateral right of divorce
entirely dependent on the husband's caprice."[23]
—J. JEREMIAS

Jesus came on the scene one generation after Hillel and Shammai. In Matthew 19:3 when the Pharisees asked Jesus the question, "Is it lawful for a man to divorce his wife for any and every reason?" they were in effect asking Him if He sided with Hillel or Shammai on the issue of divorce. Can a man divorce his wife, abandon her, and leave her liable and vulnerable simply because she burned the bread?

This wasn't only a question of divorce—it was a gender-specific question. For what reason(s) can a *man* divorce his *wife*. Jesus sided with Shammai on this issue of divorce and generously lifted women up in His first-century world. In siding with Shammai, Jesus protected women from being so easily divorced and cast aside at a husband's caprice.

Jesus brought justice and righteousness to woman within the marriage relationship—protecting her, establishing her, and rejecting the idea that a man could divorce his wife for any reason. As we'll continue to see, Jesus advocated for women who were overlooked by society. He reached out with radical kindness and grace, and in doing so, He changed their lives.

GENEROUSLY LIFTED UP

He told her, "Go, call your husband and come back."
JOHN 4:16

Jesus met the Samaritan woman at Jacob's well at the base of Mount Gerizim. It was an ordinary day that would become extraordinary in her life and story.

> "At the beginning of the conversation [Jesus] did not make himself known to her, but she first caught sight of a thirsty man, then a Jew, then a Rabbi, afterwards a prophet, last of all the Messiah. She tried to get the better of a thirsty man, she showed dislike of the Jew, she heckled the Rabbi, she was swept off her feet by the prophet, and she adored the Christ."[24]
> —Ephrem the Syrian, Eastern Father

In this moment, Jesus named her shame, not her sin. He reached all the way into her story, saw into her soul, and likely named the hardest and most shameful thing she had ever lived through. He entered into her world with compassion and empathy. Jesus seeks to enter into your world with compassion and empathy too. Ordinary days become extraordinary when you let Jesus in to generously lift you up.

If Jesus met with you at your kitchen table this week and named your shame—your deepest point of shame in your story—what would it be?

Spend some time with Him this week, thinking and praying about that part of your story. Let Jesus name your shame and generously lift you up out of it again and anew. Feel free to use the following page to journal a prayer of praise to Him.

Gracious Heavenly Father
   I praise you for your Love and
mercy and for your faithfulness.
You alone are worthy of our praise
and I worship you!

SESSION FOUR

JESUS AND THE WOMAN AGAINST A WALL

Last week, we looked at a biblical story of Jesus bringing a generous justice and righteousness (*mishpat* and *tzedakah*) to a Samaritan woman at an ancient well dug by one of the patriarchs. Jesus named her shame and immediately began lifting her up and restoring her honor. She moved from being a lonely woman, shamed by five divorces, to a missionary who told her community about the Messiah. Last week, we saw the love of Jesus be kind.

This week, as we eat our second story of Jesus and a woman in the Bible, we will see the love of Jesus be fierce. Last week's story happened at a well. This week's story happened at a meal in a Pharisee's home, a Pharisee named Simon. We will learn about the importance of table fellowship in Jesus' world and how hospitality was one of the highest virtues or signs of honor in their culture. In other words, important stuff happened during meals in Jesus' life and ministry just as, I would argue, it does today in many cases.

Look for the justice and righteousness in this story—the way Jesus generously lifted the woman up. We take heart as daughters; if Jesus did it for her, He can certainly do it for us.

As we come to this biblical table:
What have you been thinking about since last week's feast?

How caring Jesus is
He puts Himself at our level and
humbly shares His heart,

the Chronicles of Narnia
"Beaver" character?

Who did you live like a river toward last week and share what you learned at the feast?

How did that conversation go? How did your time together challenge you or confirm what you've been learning?

We are getting ready to pull up our chairs for Session Four of this biblical feast. Remember, more than reading the Word of God, we seek to *eat* it. For many of us, the best meal we can eat is one we don't have to cook. The Scriptures are a meal prepared for us by our high and holy Father. He sets a table, prepares His Word, and meets us there—communing with us as He feeds us the Word of God. We posture ourselves to receive.

Sit back. Breathe deep. Enjoy the feast!

THE FEAST

Use the following notes and space provided during our feast teaching time. Feel free to add your own notes as you watch.

WESTERN LENS	MIDDLE EASTERN LENS
Form	Function
How? *How* did it happen?	Why? *Why* would God do that?
Understand ➜ Believe	Believe ➜ Understand
Law, Rule, Principle	Story, Narrative
What does it teach me about *me*?	What does it teach me about *God*?
Dig deep, get down in it … (Analysis—pick it apart)	Read through it … (Synthesis—bring it together)
Study to acquire *knowledge*	Posture to be *fed*

The *parashah* is the weekly portion of the Torah used in Jewish liturgy; it's given in Shabbat services on Saturdays.[1]

Jesus meets us right where we are, but He never leaves us there. Last week, Jesus met the Samaritan woman at Jacob's well. This week, we'll see Him meet a woman as she sat against a wall, in a lower social position, at a meal. The Samaritan woman left the well and was never the same. Jesus pulled this woman off the wall, generously lifted her up, and sent her away in peace.

The Middle East, both then and now, has three primary cultural norms:
☐ Honor/Shame
☐ Hospitality
☐ Communal living (we, not me)[2]

mishpat = justice
tzedakah = righteousness

Refusing someone's hospitality was very shameful in the biblical world.

Table fellowship was and is very important in the Middle East. It's one of the highest forms of social affiliation.

> In Jesus' world, the basic norms of hospitality to be provided by a host were:
> □ A kiss of welcome
> □ Washing the guest's feet with water
> □ Olive oil for the guest's hands (soap)
> □ Anointing the head of honored guests with special oils
> □ Outcasts, sinners, and the poor would sit away from the table, behind the guests, against the wall, and be fed after a meal was served.[3]

A woman's hair was very important in the biblical world, and it still is in the Middle East today. A woman's hair is her glory.

Jewish people read the Scriptures and seek to embody them, not just learn them intellectually. They want to walk scriptural truths out in their everyday lives. A *lachrymatory* (think lacrimal duct in your eye) is a tear jar or tear vase. The significance behind the use of tear jars in Jewish tradition is rooted in Psalm 56:8.

The psalms were written one thousand years before the time of Jesus. For thousands of years, Jewish women have had tear jars; they even pass them down from one generation to the next. These women collect their tears in observance of Psalm 56:8. A tear jar represents the collective, sum total of a woman's grief and sorrow.

> *parabolē*—parable[4]
> *parallēlos*—parallel[5]

A parable is a story told in the parallel. It often compares or contrasts several different things. The point of a parable is to drive you to a decision.

TO ACCESS THE VIDEO TEACHING SESSIONS, USE THE INSTRUCTIONS IN THE BACK OF YOUR BIBLE STUDY BOOK.

69

Jesus through middle eastern eyes
By "Bailey"

Abraham had just been circumcised
when the 3 strangers came.
He left his tent to invite them in
and he encouraged Sarah to bake bread
and went to the livestock + told the men
to prepare the fatted calf.
Hospitality — Family — community
— Honor or shame culture —
5 — Signs of hospitality
Kiss of welcome
wash your feet with water
Olive oil for your hands
Special oils to anoint the head of
   a special person (honored guest)
Luke 7:36 — Rabbi had to be 36 (Jesus was 30)
Pharisee —
Alabaster Jar of oil to anoint Jesus' head.

LET'S YESHIVA!

Each week we're going to take some time to *yeshiva*—to emulate the Middle Eastern communal way of discussing spiritual concepts and growing together in grace as a biblical community. Discuss the following questions with your group.

What did you just *hear* or *see* in our feast together that you want to remember?

What one thing that we learned in our feast would you want to share with others this week?

How has Jesus brought *mishpat* (justice) and *tzedakah* (righteousness) into your life this week?

Who do you know who practices excellent hospitality? In your opinion, what makes him or her so good at it?

What are some of your hospitality norms when you invite people to come into your home?

When was the last time you really allowed yourself to just pour out your heart to Jesus? To even "lose it" on Him? Is there something that keeps you from pouring your heart out to Him all the time? How can you fight against that obstacle?

DAILY BREAD

We brush our teeth every day because it is good for us and keeps us healthy. It's a practice of physical hygiene. Daily Bible reading is one way we practice spiritual hygiene. We practice certain things on a daily basis because they are spiritually good for us—they keep us spiritually healthy.

I grew up calling my daily Bible reading a "quiet time." I set this time aside to intentionally be *with* the Lord *in* the Word of God. This daily practice benefited my soul in a way similar to how daily teeth brushing benefited my health. Both are forms of hygiene.

The Jewish people use different language for their weekly Bible reading. They call it the parashah, which means *portion*.[6] They read a certain portion of the Torah, or the first five books of the Old Testament Scriptures, every week.[7]

When I think of a *portion* I often think of eating—of portion control. Last week, we learned about the Hebrew word *hagah*—to devour something like a lion eating its prey. Here again, with this word *parashah*, we see the imagery of *eating* the Scriptures. We take it in. It is sweeter than honey. It becomes part of us, "a part of our fabric," as we live forward from our feasting on the Word of God.

In our Western world, we often think of studying the Scripture, almost reading it academically at times. But the Middle Eastern way is to *sim lev*, to set the Scripture upon the heart, over and over again, so much so that it can't help but seep into your heart—to consume the Scripture so much that it becomes a part of who you are.[8] We want the answer to the question, "Where is the Word of God located?" to be "inside of me."

PARASHAH (PL. PARASHOT)

Because Torah held the primary place within all of Scripture for the Jews, after the exile they decided to commit to corporately read all five books aloud throughout the course of a year.[9]

They divided the Torah into fifty-four parashot (or sections), assigning one section of each book to be read at a certain time every year. Thus, every week a new section of Scripture would be studied all week and read aloud in the synagogue for Sabbath.

We find historical evidence for this practice in the Dead Sea Scrolls and the New Testament.[10] In Luke 4 Jesus followed up the Torah reading with a passage from Isaiah. In Acts 15:21 the Jerusalem Council mentioned how the Torah was being read in the synagogues every week.

TIME IN THE WORD SHAPES WHO YOU ARE NOW AND WHO YOU ARE BECOMING.

The way we view God's Word is really important because it affects how we know Him and how we come to grow more like Him.

We are striving to create spiritual rhythms in our lives, rather than trying to strong-arm ourselves into spiritual disciplines and checking boxes. In our approach to the Bible, and really any big question we have to answer in our lives, I find it helpful to ask, "Who do you want to be?" God can use the Bible to form you more and more into the image of Christ, if you will *sim lev*—set it on your heart over and over again so that it lives inside of you, so that it becomes a part of who you are. The outworking of growth and joy and hope in our everyday lives comes from inside, from a heart transformed by time with God in His Word. Time in the Word shapes who you are now and who you are becoming.

Take a few moments to consider how you view the Bible and if God may be challenging you to make a change.

How do you view the Bible? Something to learn? Eat?

Do you view your time in the Word as a discipline, feast, or neither? Do you view it as something you're *supposed* to do? Explain.

Who do you want to be? Is that desire reflected in the way you spend time in God's Word? Explain.

The Western Wall

WALKING IT OUT

> You have kept count of my tossings; put my tears in
> your bottle. Are they not in your record?
> **PSALM 56:8 (NRSV)**

The Psalms are a gift to us. All of Scripture is God's
message to us, but in the Psalms, God gives us language
to describe every season of life—the joys and pains.

He's giving us permission to bring our most raw emotions
and desires to Him, to pour our hearts out to Him. In the
Psalms we are instructed to give the words God has given
to us back to Him. They are the language of humanity in
every condition and in every state—lament, sadness, grief,
anger, fear, regret, worry, and so on. The Psalms are a gift
because in them the Lord equips us with the language we
need to bring to Him in prayer when we feel the full range
of human emotion. The Lord wants us to share our hearts,
our true hearts, with Him no matter what we're feeling or
thinking. He can handle us. He can handle us telling Him
the truth and the whole truth.

> "How far can we go? How much is permissible?
> The Psalms suggest that we can go *the whole way*,
> that it is *all permissible*: the praise, yes, but also the
> grief, the sorrow, the anger ..."[11]
> —Walter Brueggemann

HALAKH

In Jesus' first-century world, a
Jewish rabbi wasn't interested
in teaching philosophy or grand
ideas that float around in the
sky just for the sake of debate.
Philosophy and acquiring
knowledge was the ideal of the
Greeks, not the Jews. According
to the Greeks, education was
important because "man is the
measure of all things."[12]

For the Jews, the Lord is the
Lord of all, and all things orient
to Him. A rabbi's teachings were
crafted to show you how to
halakh (walk) the *halakha* (way or
path). A rabbi taught you how to
walk out your life in the path or
way of the Living God. It wasn't
about what you thought—it
was all about how you lived. It
wasn't what you knew—it was
about how you walked the path
of the Lord.[13]

Jewish people read the Scriptures and seek to live them out, not just know them. They want to *halakh* (walk out) the path of the Lord in accordance with His instructions and laws. When they read something in Scripture, they don't just ponder it or think about it; they act. They try to embody it in the way they live their lives, sometimes literally. They don't just believe it in their hearts; they walk it out in their actions.

Psalm 56:8 speaks of tears being collected in a bottle and of God keeping a record of the tears we've shed in this life. From the days of the Psalter, about one thousand years before the time of Jesus, some Jewish women took this passage to heart and carried in their possessions a *lachrymatory*—a tear jar to use in their worship times. The lacrimal duct in our bodies produces our tears.

These Jewish women collect their tears in their tear jars, serving as a tangible way of symbolically collecting their sorrows, sadness, grief, and hurt. They then pour the tear jar out before the Lord in an act of worship, faith, and trust. To pour out one's tear jar is to pour out one's whole heart—the sorrow, sadness, and grief. This practice is a visible way of living out—walking out—Psalm 56:8.

In Psalm 56 God gives value to our tears. He tells us He sees every hurt and every sorrow. He tells us He holds our hearts in it all; He walks through it with us. He will bring joy eventually and eternally. In a similar way, the *lachrymatory* gives value to tears. They are precious to God. They are worth recognizing, and they are worth keeping. They are worth storing up because of the One who can handle *all* our tears. The One who can hold *all* of our sadness, grief, sorrow, hurt, and pain can handle it. He can take it.

And He invites you to bring it all to Him and receive His grace and redemption. God wants to generously lift you up and restore what has been broken by this world of pain and sin.

GOD WANTS TO GENEROUSLY LIFT YOU UP AND RESTORE WHAT HAS BEEN BROKEN BY THIS WORLD OF PAIN AND SIN.

The *lachrymatory* in the photo on the following page was given to me by one of my professors in Israel. An actual archaeological artifact dating back to the first or second century AD, it was uncovered in Israel.

This tear jar most likely belonged to a Jewish woman in antiquity, maybe even in the lifetime of

Jesus' earthly ministry. She might have collected her tears in this very jar. I look at the tear jar often and wonder what her story looked like—what she experienced—her highs and lows. I wonder where she kept her jar and how often she pulled it out to collect her tears before the Lord.

Kristi's ancient tear jar

It's possible the woman in Luke 7 brought two jars to the dinner with Jesus at the home of Simon the Pharisee— two jars for two very different reasons. I think she brought an alabaster jar of expensive perfume to anoint Jesus and a tear jar to pour out her sorrows to Him. In this act of worship, it seems she was recognizing Jesus' deity, pouring out her tears to Him—the tears Psalm 56 says God sees and keeps record of.

Jesus could handle both, a mixture of anointing oil and a woman's deepest pain poured out in her tears. We can pour our whole hearts out to Jesus. We can leave it *all* before Him. We can cast it all upon Him. He can take it, and He wants to take it. When we pour out our hearts to Jesus, He begins generously lifting us up in grace and truth. Like the woman in Luke 7, He can lift us up and send us on our way in peace.

What do you think about the practice of trying to embody the Scriptures in obedience?

How does the Jewish practice of the tear jar as a form of worship speak into any misgivings you may have about bringing your grief, pain, and sorrow to God?

STARING AT GOD

READ LUKE 7:36-50.

Look at this Bible passage through the **Western lens,** asking the question, "What does this teach me about *me*?" Write down what you notice in this story.

The woman was so overcome with adoration she wept at Jesus feet.
She must have felt her inadequacies being in Jesus' presence.
She was incredibly condemned —
Jesus was her "ray of hope"

Look at this Bible passage through the **Middle Eastern lens,** asking the question, "What does this teach me about *God*?" Write down what you notice in this story.

Jesus saw her broken, repentative heart.
Jesus said her "many sins" are much forgiven. Jesus pardoned her.

Now, compare your two lists of observations above.
How are they alike?

How are they different?

What did you learn about the way you typically view Scripture?

What did you learn about this passage?

This exercise is a great way for us to see some of the differences in what we glean from Bible passages based on the way we approach them and what we look for when we read the Scriptures.

Reading a passage with the question, "What does this teach me about me?" in mind often causes us to look down and turn inward, focusing on ourselves. On the other hand, when we read a passage with the question, "What does this teach me about God?" in mind we look up and out, staring at God and glancing at our lives. When we focus on what a passage teaches us about God, we devote more of our time and attention to Him, and the cares of our lives dim in comparison. As we behold Him, we are changed. Staring at God will change us in ways focusing on ourselves never can.

Remember this phrase from the psalm of ascent that we discussed in Session Two,

> I lift up my eyes to the mountains—where does my help come from?
> My help comes from the LORD, the Maker of heaven and earth.
> **PSALM 121:1-2**

As daughters of the Living God, let's look to Him for our help, strength, and joy.

Take heart, daughter. He's for us.

TIME WITH JESUS

A woman in that town who lived a sinful life learned that Jesus was eating at the Pharisee's house, so she came there with an alabaster jar of perfume. As she stood behind him at his feet weeping, she began to wet his feet with her tears. Then she wiped them with her hair, kissed them and poured perfume on them.
LUKE 7:37-38

Jesus met this woman right where she was—relegated to a position of low esteem, to a seat against the wall, not allowed to join the table fellowship at the meal. He accepted her anointing and the tears she may have poured onto His feet. He didn't flinch when she started wiping His feet with her hair, something that would have been culturally unheard of. Jesus could handle her—*all* of her poured out onto Him. He brought a generous justice to her and sent her away in peace.

Jesus can handle you too—*all* of you poured out onto Him.

Take some time this week to get honest with Jesus.

Prioritize time alone with Him, however best suits your personality and season of life.

☐ Take a walk with Him.
☐ Make a cup of coffee, climb into your favorite chair, and talk to Him.
☐ Go for a drive with the Lord and pour your heart out to Him.
☐ Tell Him what you haven't been telling Him, what you've been holding back.
☐ Use the following page to journal your heart to the Lord.

Take a moment to pour yourself out onto Him and allow Him to generously lift you up; He will gladly receive you.

SESSION FIVE

JESUS AND THE WOMAN WITH CHUTZPAH

Last week, we looked at a second story of Jesus bringing a generous justice to a woman, a woman sitting in a place of low standing against the wall at Simon the Pharisee's home during a meal. She anointed Jesus' feet with expensive perfume and maybe even poured out the tears from her tear jar onto Jesus. Weeping, she poured out her emotions— the sorrows and joys—and her worship on Jesus, and He took it. He wanted to take it.

In the way He handled the situation, Jesus in effect rearranged the room. Simon began the meal as a gracious host, a position of honor. The woman began the meal in shame, an outcast and sinner against the wall. The story ended with Simon lowered in shame because he failed to extend hospitality to Jesus according to the cultural norms of the day. The meal ended with the woman brought near to Jesus, honored before all the dinner guests, and sent away in peace. Jesus turned the room right side up. What began high and proud was brought low; the low and humble were generously lifted high.

So far in our study together, we have seen Jesus be kind in His love to the Samaritan woman and fierce in His love for the woman at Simon's home. This week, we'll see Jesus' love for a woman be unprecedented. We will learn the importance of parables in Jesus' teaching ministry. Jesus' way of teaching was highly unusual in His world and time. He did something almost no other rabbi or Pharisee was doing in the first-century world. Jesus was generously lifting up women everywhere in the very way He shaped, formed, and delivered His rabbinic parables and stories. More on that later.

Look for the justice and righteousness in this story—the generous lifting up. We take heart as daughters. If Jesus did it for her, He can certainly do it for us.

As we come to this biblical table:
What have you been thinking about since last week's feast?

Who did you live like a river toward and share what you learned at the feast last week?

On the conference call with Siblings

How did that conversation go? How did your time together challenge you or confirm what you've been learning?

As we pull up our chairs for Session Five of this biblical feast, we are reminded that more than simply reading the Word of God to learn, we seek to eat it for a transformed heart and life. We pull our chairs up to the biblical table with confidence and faith—confidence in the Lord, our Father, who feeds His children, and faith in His goodness to make sure we are fed to the full. Take a moment to still your heart and posture yourself to receive.

Sit back. Breathe deep. Enjoy the feast!

THE FEAST

Use the following notes and space provided during our feast teaching time. Feel free to add your own notes as you watch.

WESTERN LENS	MIDDLE EASTERN LENS
Form	Function
How? *How* did it happen?	Why? *Why* would God do that?
Understand ➜ Believe	Believe ➜ Understand
Law, Rule, Principle	Story, Narrative
What does it teach me about *me*?	What does it teach me about *God*?
Dig deep, get down in it … (Analysis—pick it apart)	Read through it … (Synthesis—bring it together)
Study to acquire *knowledge*	Posture to be *fed*

"We write our afflictions on marble, our mercies upon sand."[1]
—Charles Spurgeon

In Jesus' world, rabbis and Pharisees often used parables as their primary teaching method. They would share their theologies not in terms of academic teaching—what we might think of as systematic theology—but through stories. Approximately one-third of Jesus' recorded words in the Gospels are in parabolic form.[2]

parabolē—parable
parallēlos—parallel

A parable is a story told in the parallel. It often compares and contrasts different things. The point of a parable is to drive you to a decision.

Parables were very common in Jesus' day. However, rabbis and Pharisees rarely used women as the subject matter of their parables or stories. Women were considered too lowly to communicate divine things. Parables and stories were almost always told in the masculine.

Jesus was extremely unique in that He often included women in His stories, parables, and ministry. In the Gospel of Luke, we see twenty-seven pairings of spiritual teachings and Jesus' actions. (See chart on pp. 91–93.)[3] It was not unusual for Jesus to share two stories or parables: one featuring a man, the other featuring a woman. With Jesus, women found their place in the story over and over again. Jesus brought a generous justice to women everywhere in the very way He shaped, formed, and taught His parables. When Jesus wanted to teach a parable about praying with persistence, He could have used several historical and biblically important characters, for example:

- ☐ Abraham praying and contending for Sodom and Gomorrah (Gen. 18).
- ☐ Jacob wrestling with the angel of the Lord at the river Jabbok (Gen. 32).
- ☐ Moses praying for God's anger to turn from the idolatrous Israelites (Ex. 32).
- ☐ Hannah praying for a child during her years of barrenness (1 Sam. 1).

Instead, Jesus cast a widow woman as the main character of His parable (Luke 18:1-8). This widow began the story at the bottom, powerless against an unrighteous judge. But she ended the story on top, having bent the will of the unrighteous judge with her *chutzpah* (persistence in coming to him over and over again).[4]

Journaling is a great way to record our very own God stories. Remembering is a spiritual practice in the Middle East. It's good to take time to write down, remember, and celebrate God's activity in our lives.

In our biblical feast two weeks ago, we saw Jesus meet the Samaritan woman at Jacob's well. In last week's feast, He pulled a woman off the wall, honored her publicly, and sent her away in peace. In this week's feast, Jesus used not just any woman, but a widow woman, to teach His disciples "they should always pray and not give up" (Luke 18:1).

TO ACCESS THE VIDEO TEACHING SESSIONS, USE THE INSTRUCTIONS IN THE BACK OF YOUR BIBLE STUDY BOOK.

87

Somewhat unprecedented

Stories were shared in parables

Mashal - Parabolic teaching

1/3 of Jesus' words are in a parable form.

Jesus did something as He taught

He taught 2 at a time - 1 masculine +

1 feminine.. When Jesus talks,

women are included.

Parable of mending a tear with fabric

+ mending wineskin with a patch.

Parable of the lost sheep + lost coin.

↓ Parable of the good shepherd

2nd - Parable of the good woman

3rd Parable of the running father

Because of this we should better know

who the loving God is.

Luke 13:18-21 Men + women mentioned.

27 pairings in Luke alone

Luke 18:1-8

Pray + don't give up.

chutzpah is persistance in prayer

Jesus used a woman (+ a widow) in this
story that gives a widow honor.

Faith of the centurion   Matt 8:5-11
the lack of faith in Nazareth   Mark 6

LET'S YESHIVA!

Each week we're going to take some time to *yeshiva*—to emulate the Middle Eastern communal way of discussing spiritual concepts and growing together in grace as a biblical community. Discuss the following questions with your group.

What did you just *hear* or *see* in our feast together that you want to remember? *Pray with Persistance -*

What one thing that we learned in our feast would you want to share with others this week? *Faith or Lack of Faith?*

How has Jesus brought *mishpat* (justice) and *tzedakah* (righteousness) into your life this week? Describe the situation to your group.

Remembering was a spiritual rhythm and practice in the biblical world, and it's still a common practice in the Middle Eastern world today. What are some of your rhythms of *remembering* so you don't forget the things the Lord has done for you? If you don't have any, what new rhythms could you start practicing?

How long do you pray for something before you give up? Before you quit? Explain.

How does it make you feel to realize that Jesus was adamant about including women in His stories and parables?

If Jesus were to be amazed at you right now, would it be for your faith or lack of faith? What circumstances are challenging your faith right now? What situations are encouraging your faith right now?

You may want to split up into smaller groups to ask this last question since it's a bit more personal.

What are the unmet longings in your life? The things you long for that haven't come to fruition? Is it hard to keep praying on and on for those things? Have you let them go? Let them die? What would it look like for you to resurrect those prayers for that thing? To pray with *chutzpah* yet again for it?

THE TEACHINGS OF JESUS

Jesus was *adamant* about including women. The following chart shows the way that Jesus made a point of including both women and men in His spiritual teachings and His earthly ministry, an unheard of practice in His day.

PAIRINGS IN THE GOSPEL OF LUKE

MASCULINE	FEMININE
Gabriel appears to Zechariah (1:8-23)	Gabriel appears to Mary (1:26-38)
Song of Zechariah (1:67-79)	Song of Mary (1:46-55)
Simeon encounters Baby Jesus in the temple (2:25-35)	Anna encounters Baby Jesus in the temple (2:36-38)
Naaman and Israelite lepers (4:27)	Widow of Zarephath and Israelite widows (4:25-26)
Healing of demon-possessed man in Capernaum (4:31-37)	Healing of Simon's mother-in-law in Capernaum (4:38-39)
The parable of new wine in new wineskins (5:37-39)	The parable of sewing a patch on old clothes (5:36)
Naming of twelve apostles (6:12-16)	Naming of the women who were with Jesus (8:1-3)
Centurion's servant is healed (7:1-10)	Widow of Nain's son raised from the dead (7:11-17)
The parable of men who each owed a debt (7:41-43)	Jesus forgives a sinful woman (7:36-50)

MASCULINE	FEMININE
Jesus traveled with the Twelve (8:1)	Some women who had been healed also traveled with Jesus (8:2)
Fear addressed—disciples in a boat during a storm (8:22-25)	Fear addressed—Jairus's daughter healed (8:41-42,49-56)
Healing of demon-possessed man in Gerasenes (8:26-39)	Healing of a bleeding woman (8:43-48)
The parable of the good Samaritan (10:25-37)	Example of Mary choosing to sit at Jesus' feet (10:38-42)
Family divided: father versus son (12:52-53)	Family divided: mother versus daughter (12:52-53)
Sick man healed (14:1-6)	Crippled woman healed (13:10-17)
The parable of a man planting a mustard seed (13:18-19)	The parable of a woman mixing yeast and flour (13:20-21)
The parable of the lost son (15:11-32)	The parable of the woman looking for a lost coin (15:8-10)
The parable of the shrewd manager taking advantage of position (16:1-15)	Teaching on divorce—men taking advantage of women (16:18)
Two men sleeping, one taken (17:34)	Two women grinding meal, one taken (17:35)
Rich young ruler won't receive kingdom (18:18-30)	(Likely) Women bringing children to Jesus—theirs is the kingdom (18:15-17)
The parable of the Pharisee and the tax collector—prayer (18:9-14)	The parable of the persistent widow—prayer (18:1-8)

MASCULINE	FEMININE
Rich Pharisees giving in the temple treasury (20:45–21:1)	The poor widow giving two copper coins (21:2-4)
Last days—men will faint from terror (21:26)	Last days—dreadful for nursing and pregnant mothers (21:23)
Two men question Peter (22:58-59)	Servant girl questions Peter (22:56-57)
Simon of Cyrene carries Jesus' cross (23:26)	Jesus meets women on way to Calvary (23:27-29)
Joseph of Arimathea buries Jesus' body (23:50-53)	Women see where Jesus is buried (23:55-56)
Resurrection evidence—two men on way to Emmaus (24:13-35)	Resurrection evidence—women see angels at empty tomb (24:1-8)

In the first-century world, before Jesus upended things, all spiritual teaching was for men. Imagine, as a woman, hearing the teaching of God's Word with your family, to only find spiritual application directed at your male relatives. We have so much access to spiritual teaching today, it's easy to take it for granted. For a moment, though, put yourself in the shoes of the first-century Jewish woman.

> What do you imagine it would have been like to have no spiritual teaching directed to you? How do you think it would have affected your spiritual growth and your attitude toward God?

Feeling neglected – condesending

In His approach to teaching and His earthly ministry, Jesus said to women in the first century—you are a part of this story, too. You matter. You're seen by God. You're prized by God. You're in His story. God is calling you to be a part of His kingdom work. And Jesus is saying that to us as women today too.

The point of a parable is to drive you to a decision.

In the parable of the persistent widow in Luke 18, for example, the text challenges our understanding of why and how we should pray. Parables are meant to spur action; again, here we see the Middle Eastern idea of obedience to God's Word through embodiment. We don't simply read His Word; we walk it out. We make His Word a part of who we are, so much so that it shapes the way we think and act day in and day out.

Pick two of the pairings in the chart on pages 91–93. As you read both passages in each pair, record below what you think the parables/stories teach and the decision you think the parables/stories drive you toward.

Pairing:
Naming of 12 apostles
Naming of women with Jesus

What the parables/stories teach:
Same importance of men + women

Decision the parables/stories drive you toward:

Pairing:
Gabriel appears to Zechariah
+ Gabriel appears to Mary

What the parables/stories teach:
The same treatment of men + women.

Decision the parables/stories drive you toward:

ZAKHAR

We have spiritual disciplines and practices as New Testament believers. We do certain things as Christians to live out our faith. When I hear the phrase *spiritual disciplines*, lots of things come to mind such as Bible study, prayer, attending a local church, tithing, living missionally, and serving others.

Throughout time, the Jewish people have also had their own spiritual rhythms and practices—some similar to ours and some unique to their faith. In the Bible we see God issue many commandments, but He repeats one of them over and over—"remember" and "do not forget."

The Lord knows we are a forgetful people. I often forget where I put my car keys. I walk into a room sometimes and forget why I went there in the first place! We are equally forgetful, if not more so, when it comes to our spiritual lives. We tend to have spiritual amnesia. We easily forget the things the Lord has done for us—His faithful record over the course of our whole lives.

Instead, we tend to remember our traumas, our hurts, the things that have devastated us and left us reeling, trying to catch our breath. We often forget the blessings—the beautiful things and the grace-filled moments when the Lord has provided healing, restoration, redemption, grace, direction, or divine intervention.

The Hebrew word *zakhar* means "to remember."[5]

We typically conceive of remembering as looking back or thinking back to something in the past. But in the Hebrew culture, remembering is actually considered a forward-moving practice. Remembering is the way to move

IF YOU COME TO A PLACE OR A TIME WHEN YOU AREN'T SURE WHERE TO GO OR WHAT TO DO NEXT, PAUSE AND LOOK BACK. REMEMBER HOW THE LORD MET YOU, DIRECTED YOU, AND PROVIDED FOR YOU IN THOSE PAST TIMES.

forward, to step into the unknown future. Biblical remembering, or *zakhar*, carries this same idea of forward motion.

Here's how it practically plays out. If you come to a place or a time when you aren't sure where to go or what to do next, pause and look back. Remember how the Lord met you, directed you, and provided for you in those past times.

Remembering God's faithful record in our lives gives us courage to trust Him in the unknown and live forward. We *zakhar* (remember) so that we can step forward, because the same God who was faithful to be with us in the past is the God who will be faithful to be with us in a future that may seem unknown. We don't remember for remembering sake, but we remember to move forward with renewed faith and hope in the God who is shepherding our whole lives.

We can practice *zakhar* both personally and communally.

In the Jewish feasts and festivals, God prescribed corporate occasions for remembering. In these festivals, the Jewish people come together to remember and retell their God stories to their children. They come together to celebrate God's faithfulness in their lives and in their stories. Remembering always brings celebration because God has *never* failed us—His record is 100 percent.

> Take a moment to brainstorm and consider a few spiritual practices of remembering you could add to your life, both personal and communal. Record them below.

My personal remembering rhythm is journaling. My communal remembering rhythm is inviting people to come sit around my firepit with me as we tell our God stories by firelight. They both allow me to rehearse God's goodness and give Him glory in the seasons of ease and difficulty. Feel free to give them a try.

IT'S ALL ABOUT PERSPECTIVE

In Luke 15 Jesus shares a parable made up of three different stories. It's like a series of three pearls strung together to share the beautiful truth of how the Lord comes looking for us when we are lost, how He comes to bring us home. He truly comes to seek (go looking for) and save (bring home) the lost.

Throughout the history of the canon of Scripture, as the Bible was adapted into different languages and arranged, editors added chapter and verse labels along with the subheading descriptions you see in your Bibles to aid readers in locating and citing portions of the Scriptures.[6]

The subheadings and story titles often reflect our Western lens, one that asks, "What does this passage teach me about *me*?"

But, in the Middle East, the same passages of Scripture often have different subheadings and story titles, descriptions that reflect the Middle Eastern lens, asking, "What does this teach me about *God*?"

Let's use Luke 15 as an example of how our lens so often determines what we are looking for or focusing on in a passage of Scripture.

READ LUKE 15.

 Look at this Bible passage through the **Western lens,** asking the question, "What does this teach me about *me*?" Write down what you notice in these stories.

We look for the one and leave the others
the joy of finding what's lost.
Rejoicing is stressed —
God searches for us too + rejoices when
we come to Him,
He rejoices over us when we come to Him,

Look at this Bible passage through the **Middle Eastern lens,** asking the question, "What does this teach me about *God*?" Write down what you notice in these stories.

He rejoices over us when we come to Him.

The chart below details the subheadings that accompany these Luke 15 stories in the Western Bible versus the Middle Eastern text.

LUKE 15 DESCRIPTIONS

WEST	MIDDLE EAST
The parable of the lost sheep	The parable of the good shepherd
The parable of the lost coin	The parable of the good woman
The parable of the lost son[7]	The parable of the running father[8]

Would you rather read a story about a lost sheep or a good shepherd? Would you rather read a story about a lost coin or a good woman? Would you rather read a story about a lost son or a running father who goes to find his lost son?

Having read the passage, which of the descriptions resonates with you more? *Lost coin is easy to associate with.*

Reading the Bible with a Middle Eastern lens helps us to learn to stare at God and glance at our lives. It prompts us to pivot our gaze and the focus of our hearts off of ourselves and circumstances and instead fix our eyes on God, His work, His faithfulness, His goodness, and His generous justice in our lives. Notice Jesus used a woman as the main character in the second story here in Luke 15. Her story sets up the famous parable of the prodigal son or, as I prefer to call it, the parable of the running father.

YOUR GOD STORIES

Jesus loved using women in His stories and parables. He wanted to make sure women knew they had and have a place, an important place, in the story of the Bible and the redemptive, restorative flow of human history.

Your stories matter. Your story matters. The little stories and the big story. All of it. The up, down, and all around of your life. It all matters to Jesus. Since Jesus used women in His stories and parables, we should be women who share our stories to bless, encourage, edify, challenge, and strengthen others. Plus, our stories give glory to God. It's a win-win.

What are some of the most important God stories in your own life? Write one or two below.

profound protection when I didn't realize I was in danger. Divine intervention.

Have you ever written them down before or shared them with other people? Why or why not?

What would it look like for you to both personally and communally *zakhar* (remember)?

SESSION SIX

JESUS AND THE WOMAN ON THE SOUTHERN STEPS

So far we have seen the love of Jesus be kind to the Samaritan woman. His love was fierce for the woman at Simon's home. And last week, we saw an unprecedented display of the love of Jesus for woman, when He featured a widow woman as the main character in His parable about learning to pray without giving up. Jesus was bringing justice (*mishpat*) and righteousness (*tzedakah*) to women everywhere in the very way He created, shaped, formed, and taught His parables and stories.

This week, we'll see the epic love of Jesus for woman. We'll eat an electric story that reaches deep, high, and wide in its scope. This week's biblical story centers on Jesus and the woman caught in adultery. Today we see what Jesus would do with a sinful woman. Again, we will watch as Jesus brought a generous justice to a woman. She would learn to take heart as a daughter and to live forward as one covered, lifted, and released in peace.

Look for the justice and righteousness in this story—the generous lifting up. We take heart as daughters. If Jesus did it for her, He can certainly do it for us.

As we come to this biblical table:
What have you been thinking about since last week's feast?

Jesus loves women – In heaven
there will be no male/female

Who did you live like a river toward and share what you learned at the feast last week?

My siblings —

How did that conversation go? How did your time together challenge you or confirm what you've been learning?

Jesus is amazed by faith and lack of faith.

Zakhar — Remember!

We are getting ready to pull up our chairs for Session Six of this biblical feast. We are getting ready to eat the biblical meal prepared for us by our Father. He feeds. We receive. We are postured to stare at Him and glance at our lives. When we stare at our problems, they become giants in our eyes. When we stare at God, our problems take on their proper scope and perspective. We are not left to ourselves to find our way home. The Lord will take His Word and break it down for us today in bite-size pieces. We are a saved people. We are also a fed people.

Sit back. Breathe deep. Enjoy the feast!

THE FEAST

Use the following notes and space provided during our feast teaching time. Feel free to add your own notes as you watch.

WESTERN LENS	MIDDLE EASTERN LENS
Form	Function
How? *How* did it happen?	Why? *Why* would God do that?
Understand ➜ Believe	Believe ➜ Understand
Law, Rule, Principle	Story, Narrative
What does it teach me about *me*?	What does it teach me about *God*?
Dig deep, get down in it … (Analysis—pick it apart)	Read through it … (Synthesis—bring it together)
Study to acquire *knowledge*	Posture to be *fed*

More Athens+Rome
than Jerusalem

Three weeks ago, we feasted on the story of Jesus meeting the Samaritan woman at Jacob's well. Two weeks ago, we saw Him pull the woman off the wall at Simon the Pharisee's home, honoring her publicly and sending her away in peace. Last week, we rejoiced as we saw Jesus create and shape a parable about a widow upending an unjust judge with her persistence, bending his will until he granted her request. This type of teaching was highly unusual since rabbis and religious leaders didn't usually include women as the subject matter of their stories and parables.

This week, we're going to discuss what Jesus did with a sinful woman, a woman caught in the act of adultery.

Several early manuscripts and many other ancient witnesses do not include the text of John 7:53–8:11.

In Deuteronomy 16 the Lord commanded three annual pilgrimage festivals. They are also called *foot festivals*. Jews from around the world came to Jerusalem three times a year for these celebrations. The festivals are called Passover (in the spring), the Feast of Weeks or Pentecost (in the spring), and the Feast of Tabernacles (in the fall).[1] These seven-day celebrations in Jerusalem commemorated God's faithfulness in the lives of His people.

This week's story happened on the eighth day, the day after the seven-day Festival of Tabernacles ended. The eighth day was designated as a "sabbath" (Lev. 23:36). After seven days of celebrating God's faithfulness, you need to *rest*.

> *Mishnah* on Sabbath:
> ☐ Writing that leaves a permanent mark (ink on papyrus, etc.) was work.
> ☐ Writing with your finger in dust, sand, or dirt (blows away) was accepted.[2]

Jesus was known as a Galilean Rabbi, or a Rabbi of the North.[3] Most of His earthly ministry happened in the northern district of Galilee. This week's story happened down south, in the district of Judea. It happened *in* Jerusalem, *at* the temple after the fall Festival of Tabernacles—a highly public moment with everyone there in the temple, including Jews from around the world.

The Pharisees brought in a woman caught in adultery. Where was the man? They were not honestly concerned with the Law being broken, or they would have brought the man involved in the adultery too. They were trying to trap Jesus in a public moment with lots of people around. The *first* time Jesus wrote in the sand (honoring Sabbath regulations about writing), scholars believe He most likely wrote Leviticus 20:10 in response to their question about the Law of Moses concerning adultery.[4] Jesus' next words were about who would stone the

SABBATH

Many of us understand the idea of Sabbath in the context of a day of rest, set aside to worship God. And Sabbath is anchored in the God-given gift of rest. But it's more than rest— it's centered in a restful celebration of restoration.

The creation account in Genesis 1 and 2 shows the Lord ordering, organizing, and putting things in their right places. The creation account is a restorative creation; the Lord was creating and shaping things in *shalom*. Throughout Jesus' earthly ministry, He celebrates Sabbath by bringing restoration. He loves to heal on the Sabbath. In doing so, He is not acting contrary to God's Sabbath command. He is actually mirroring His Father's character, being like His Father, setting things right—the way they were meant to be.

TO ACCESS THE VIDEO TEACHING SESSIONS, USE THE INSTRUCTIONS IN THE BACK OF YOUR BIBLE STUDY BOOK.

105

woman—the penalty for adultery in the Law of Moses. Jesus said the ones among them without sin should be first to throw a stone at her.

The *second* time Jesus wrote in the sand (honoring Sabbath regulations about writing), scholars believe He may have begun writing the names of the Pharisees standing around Him in the sand, in reference to Jeremiah 17:13—a passage about dishonest shepherds not leading the people of Israel well.[5] In other words, these men were *not* without sin. Instead, they had forsaken the Lord; they were sinful.

> "LORD, you are the hope of Israel; all who forsake you will be put to shame. Those who turn away from you will be written in the dust because they have forsaken the LORD, the spring of living water."
> JEREMIAH 17:13

When Jesus started writing their names, the religious leaders began walking away. Jesus had shifted their wrath off of the woman and onto Himself. The Pharisees started out mad at her, and they walked away mad at Him for calling them out. Once they had all walked away, only Jesus and the woman were there. In my opinion, whether she knew it or not, this was actually the scariest moment for the woman. Jesus was sinless. He was the only one who could have justly thrown the stone if He chose to do so.

Jesus told the woman He would not condemn her.

Jesus atoned for (covered) her sin, her shame, and generously lifted her up. He literally saved her life from the religious leaders who would certainly have stoned her to death if it were left up to them.

Justice + Righteousness
Mishpath + Tzedakah

Matt, Mark, Luke were written first — then
John — He added 7:53 — 8:11
John wrote his last — so this story was
not included in the 1st 3 gospels
Deut. 16 — 7 day feasts + festivals
① Passover — (Pentecost) ② Feast of weeks
③ Feast of Tabernacles   John 7:37-38
Isaiah 55:1
After the 7 day feast — on the 8th day — ink
wasn't allowed because it was considered
work — but Jesus wrote in the dust/sand
because the wind would blow it away.
Leviticus 20:10 —

LET'S YESHIVA!

Each week we're going to take some time to *yeshiva*—to emulate the Middle Eastern communal way of discussing spiritual concepts and growing together in grace as a biblical community. Discuss the following questions with your group.

What did you just *hear* or *see* in our feast together that you want to remember?

What one thing that we learned in our feast would you want to share with others this week?

How has Jesus brought *mishpat* (justice) and *tzedakah* (righteousness) into your life this week?

Now that you know the historical and cultural context of the story of the woman caught in adultery, why do you think the earliest manuscripts didn't have this passage recorded? Why might it have taken a while for this story to make it into the canon of the Bible?

What do you think of Susanna Wesley's definition of sin, "[Take this rule.] Whatever weakens your reason, impairs the tenderness of your conscience, obscures your sense of God, or takes off your relish of spiritual things; in short, whatever increases the strength of authority of your body over your mind; that thing is sin to you, however innocent it may be in itself"?[6] How would you define sin?

SHIFTING OUR GAZE

On any given day we are usually spending most of our time staring at one thing and glancing at everything else in our lives. Something has our attention. Something is on our minds.

When we stare at our lives and glance at God, the troubles and problems in our lives can begin to look huge. If we're not careful, our problems take up most of the space in our thoughts and consequently govern our hearts and emotions.

When we intentionally focus our minds and hearts on God, our troubles take on their proper perspective. God helps us to see them in light of His generous justice, His generous lifting up in our lives.

What are you currently staring at in your life?

WHEN WE INTENTIONALLY FOCUS OUR MINDS AND HEARTS ON GOD, OUR TROUBLES TAKE ON THEIR PROPER PERSPECTIVE.

What troubles or problems seem huge as you stare at them?

What would it look like for you to consider that trouble, that problem, up against God—His love, power, and wisdom?

Having considered your problem in light of who God is and what He says about you, what does it look like to you now?

WHERE JESUS WALKED

People often ask me which sites and places in Israel are my favorite to visit when I take teams there. It's such a hard question for me to answer because I love every inch of the land. I'm amazed as I stand in places where the biblical stories actually happened. The Bible becomes 3-D. As I am visiting these locations, the Bible passages shift from black and white to color for me. There is such a big difference in reading the Bible and beholding these places for yourself.

The Southern Rabbinic Teaching Steps

Our story this week almost certainly occurred on the Southern Rabbinic Teaching Steps at the temple in Jerusalem. Sometimes today these teaching steps are called the Southern Steps. If you go to Israel, you simply *must* go sit on those steps. Why?

You must visit these steps because Jesus walked them, and He walked these very steps often. It's one place where we *know* He spent time. So did Joseph, Mary, Peter, John, James, Stephen, Paul, Silas, Barnabas, Timothy, and many other people we read about in the pages of Scripture. I love sitting on those steps with teams, taking the scene in, reading the stories that happened right there and imagining how it all must have played out.

Three Annual Pilgrimage Festivals

> Three times a year all your men must appear before the LORD your God at the place he will choose: at the Festival of Unleavened Bread [Passover], the Festival of Weeks [Pentecost] and the Festival of Tabernacles.
> **DEUTERONOMY 16:16a**

In Torah, the Lord commanded the Jewish people to come to Jerusalem, to His house (temple) three times a year for the festivals and feasts, also known as the pilgrimage festivals or foot festivals. We've talked about them briefly already.

In these seven-day festivals, Jewish people came to Jerusalem from all over to celebrate God's faithfulness *with* Him at His house. They collectively and communally remembered God's faithful provision for them over the past year and celebrated together.

As pilgrims arrived at God's house (temple) and ascended the Southern Steps, they possibly sang the psalms of ascent (Pss. 120–134) in anticipation of going into God's house to worship, remember, and celebrate together.[7] The steps were arranged in an irregular fashion, both the original stones and the stones that have been replaced since then. The height and width of the stairs were not consistent. They were specifically designed to make the pilgrim think and consider the solemnity of worship and going before God as he or she ascended to the Huldah Gates to enter the temple.

You can just imagine the way Jerusalem would have come alive during the three annual festivals—the hustle and bustle, the throngs of people, the chatter and laughter and merriment—a people celebrating the faithfulness of their God with Him at His house.

Daily Life on the Southern Steps in Jesus' First-Century World

The Southern Rabbinic Teaching Steps were also where Pharisees and rabbis taught their disciples (*talmidim*) during the first-century world of Jesus. Rabbis did not teach inside the temple. The temple was reserved for worship, prayer, and sacrifice. Teaching happened on the Southern Steps.

Rabbis and Pharisees also discussed, debated, and shared their teachings with one another on those steps. Remember, our story this week took place on the eighth day after the fall Festival of Tabernacles; everyone had been in Jerusalem for the foot festival. The day after the Festival of Tabernacles ended, Jesus went back to the temple to teach.[8]

TALMID

In the first-century world, a disciple (*talmid*) wanted to be just like his rabbi.[9] A *talmid* didn't want to know what his rabbi knew—the *talmid* wanted to *be like* the rabbi.

People chose their rabbis in Jesus' world. You would listen to a rabbi over time, and if you agreed with the way he interpreted Scripture and respected his leadership, you would ask if you could follow him—if you could be one of his *talmidim* (disciples).[10]

Jesus was revolutionary when He came on the scene because He reached out to certain people and chose them as His disciples. When He chose them, in the culture of the day He was implicitly saying, "I think you can be just like me."

Later, Jesus told His disciples they would do greater things than He had done (John 14:12). How can this be? He knew they would go into the world in multiplied fashion, serving the world as His disciples— He knew they would go be just like Him as the Spirit of God enabled them throughout the world.

Then they all went home, but Jesus went to the Mount of Olives. At dawn he appeared again in the temple courts, where all the people gathered around him, and he sat down to teach them. The teachers of the law and the Pharisees brought in a woman caught in adultery.
JOHN 7:53–8:3a

Jesus was probably sitting on the Southern Steps, teaching His *talmidim* (disciples) when the religious leaders brought in a woman caught in the act of adultery.

READ JOHN 8:3-11.

Every time I sit on those steps, I think of her. What she must have experienced that day some two thousand years ago—the public humiliation, her sin named out loud for all the pilgrims to hear. Her terror because she knew the penalty for adultery in her world was stoning. She probably believed she would not see the sun set that night. I wonder while she stood there, taking it all in, taking it in for what might possibly be the last time, what was she thinking about? Her family? Her children? How badly the rocks would hurt hitting her hard as they were hurled down at her in a ravine? Would it be a slow death or a quick one? I wonder what her prayer sounded like in that moment.

Jesus atoned for (covered) her, generously lifted her up out of her sin and shame and sent her away in peace—encouraging her to live forward in a new way.

Go now and leave your life of sin.
JOHN 8:11b

What about this story in John 8 fuels your worship of Jesus?

Neil Armstrong, the first man to ever step foot onto the moon, visited Israel one year and went to the Southern Steps. When he learned that Jesus had walked on those very steps so often during His earthly life and ministry, Armstrong said, "I am more excited stepping on these stones than I was stepping on the moon."[11]

SEEKING SHALOM

Our story this week ends with Jesus sending the woman caught in adultery away, generously lifted up with the encouragement to go and leave her life of sin.

In essence, sin means to "miss the mark."[12] It's an archery term. The laws of God help us to hit the mark. The Hebrew word for "law" in the Old Testament is *yarah,* and it means "instructions."[13] God gives us instructions in His laws. Instructions for what? What mark are we trying to hit? What mark do we miss when we sin?

We often think of the opposite of sin as righteousness or cleanness. This is a right understanding, so we want to hang onto it. While keeping this understanding in mind, we also want to expand our understanding and look at these things in the greater meta-narrative, or flow, of the big story of the Bible.

The garden of Eden was created in *shalom*, a Hebrew word that means wholeness, harmony, flourishing, and delight.[14] Most people hear the word *shalom* and immediately think of peace. But in Hebrew, *shalom* means much more than peace. As Cornelius Plantinga Jr. puts it, "Shalom … is the way things ought to be."[15]

In Genesis 3, Adam and Eve ate the forbidden fruit and sin entered the world, the Story. *Shalom* was disturbed and thrown off balance because sin messes up the way things were meant to be. We were created for Eden but find ourselves living in a broken world, where sin still disturbs *shalom*. We all ache for Eden; we long for home.

YARAH

When we see the word *law,* it can bring up thoughts of rules and regulations— things we are penalized for if we break them (think of something like a speeding ticket).

The word *law* in the Old Testament is the Hebrew word *yarah.* Contrary to our Western idea of law, the word *yarah* carries the idea of instructions.

God's laws are His instructions. Instructions for what?

For how to live in *shalom.*

God gives us instructions to help us hit the mark, to live in *shalom*—the abundant life He desires for us.

We might shy away from *law,* but we love *instructions* for living in *shalom*. This is the psalmist's delight in Psalm 119 when he writes of his love for the laws of God because they show us the path for flourishing that God has mapped out for us.

"Sin is the missing of a target, a wandering from the path, a straying from the fold. Sin is a hard heart and a stiff neck. Sin is blindness and deafness. It is both the overstepping of a line and a failure to reach it—both transgression and shortcoming … sin is never normal. Sin is disruption of created harmony and then resistance to divine restoration of that harmony."[16]
—Cornelius Plantinga Jr.

The opposite of sin is *shalom*—the way God created things to be. The Lord doesn't hate sin because we broke a rule, law, or instruction. The Lord hates sin because sin disturbs our *shalom*. It disrupts our harmony, wholeness, flourishing, delight, and communion with God. It disrupts the way God created us to be—in relationship with Him and with one another. In encouraging the woman in our story this week to leave her life of sin, Jesus was inviting her into *shalom*—a renewed sense of the harmony, wholeness, flourishing, and delight the Lord wished for her to know and experience in her life.

How would you define *sin*?

When you sin or break the law/*yarah* of the Lord, how do you feel?

How do you feel when you confess, repent, and move back toward *shalom*?

If this definition of *shalom* is new for you, how might an understanding of this biblical concept shape your view of God and how you live forward?

READ JOHN 21:4-19.

Look at this Bible passage through the **Western lens,** asking the question, "What does this teach me about *me*?" (This would cause us to focus on Peter in the story.) Write down what you notice in this story.

Look at this Bible passage through the **Middle Eastern lens,** asking the question, "What does this teach me about *God*?" (This would cause us to focus on Jesus in the story.) Write down what you notice in this story.

You may remember part of Peter's story. Jesus prophesied that Peter would deny any affiliation with Jesus among the crowds before His crucifixion. Though Peter vehemently asserted he would never do such a thing, we see him deny Jesus three times in John 18, just as Jesus foretold. In the John 21 passage that we just read, we believe we're reading the account of Peter seeing the resurrected Jesus for the third time.

Many scholars believe John 21 took place in a location in Israel that is now called the Primacy of Peter, a place where waterfalls come together into springs. Jewish fishermen often used this location to wash their nets. We also believe that this location is where Jesus called Peter and his brother Andrew to follow Jesus in the first place.[17] If that is true, we imagine this location must have held some significant memories for Peter. Fishing there, he may have remembered the day that Jesus, one of the most famous rabbis, chose him. With those happy memories would have likely come a pang of guilt and anxiety about betraying Jesus.

But Jesus meets us where we are and never leaves us there. Imagine the scene here: Peter saw the post-resurrection Lord, immediately stopped what he was doing, threw on his garment, and jumped in the water to get to Jesus as fast as he could. Peter saw Jesus, who called him, chose him, whom he rejected. And that same Jesus who called Peter to follow Him those years ago, called Peter to the table, a place of restoration, a place of communal love and affiliation.

The Jews believe that much of life is cyclical, and this story is no exception. The place of Peter's calling was also the place of his restoration, the place where Jesus brought back his *shalom*, the place where Jesus provided missional vision for the rest of Peter's life.

We may all have a moment like this with Jesus one day, a moment where we know we've blown it and Jesus graciously restores our fellowship with Him—moving us forward into *shalom*, moving us forward into purpose for Him. When we come to Jesus, we lose our lives, but God just keeps giving more and more. He keeps generously lifting us up to love and know Him. God is better than we ever knew.

EPIC LOVE

Everything about this week's biblical story is epic—the public nature of the incident, the fact that it happened in Jerusalem the day after a seven-day festival, the intent of the religious leaders to lay a trap for Jesus, the grave nature of the woman's sin with a penalty of stoning in the Torah, and the fact that Jesus was sitting on the Southern Steps teaching His disciples when the religious leaders brought the sinful woman before Him.

The love of Jesus for the woman was also epic. He shifted the wrath of the Pharisees off of her and turned it onto Himself—to the point that they walked away mid-story, mid-moment. Jesus atoned for (covered) the woman's sin and shame; He saved her life and sent her away in peace.

The love of God for you is epic. If you are a follower of Christ, He has shifted the wrath of your enemies onto Himself, atoned for your sin and shame, and sent you away in peace—to walk the path of *shalom* in renewed life and service to Him, much as He did for this woman.

What have been the most epic moments of your life?

What have been the most significant seasons in your life?

How have you experienced sin disturbing *shalom* in your life?

Is there anything disturbing your *shalom* right now? Explain.

Do not be afraid to name the thing disturbing your *shalom* and confess it to Jesus. His love for you is epic—He will cover, forgive, and send you forward in *shalom*. He will generously lift you up.

JESUS AND THE TALE OF TWO MARYS

So far we have seen the love of Jesus be kind to the Samaritan woman. His love was fierce for the woman at Simon's home. His love for women was unprecedented in the way He shaped and formed His stories and parables to intentionally include women. Jesus made a clear point when He shaped a story with a widow as the central character, a widow whose persistence was enough to upend an unjust judge. Jesus brought justice (*mishpat*) and righteousness (*tzedakah*) to women everywhere in the very way He created, shaped, formed, and taught His parables and stories, and in the way He lived His life.

Last week, we saw the epic love of Jesus for the woman caught in adultery. We saw what Jesus did with a sinful woman—He atoned for her, generously lifted her up, and then sent her away with an invitation to live away from sin and toward *shalom*. Again we saw Jesus bring generous justice to a woman.

This week, we will focus on two women whose stories we read in the Bible and their relationships to Jesus. We will see what are, in my opinion, one of the hardest yeses a person in the Bible ever gave to the Lord and one of the most unique yeses a person in the Bible ever gave to Jesus. Hint: they were both given by women! We will also head toward the finish line for our series by looking at how we can take heart today as God's daughters and live our lives from that posture.

This seven-week feast is showing us how Jesus brought justice (*mishpat*) and righteousness (*tzedakah*) to women in His first-century world. In every story, He was generously lifting them up, restoring their honor. They were learning to take heart as daughters. We are reading these stories again and anew with Middle Eastern eyes, seeing them anchored in their historical, cultural, linguistic, and geographic context.

Look for the justice and righteousness in these stories this week—the generous lifting up. We take heart as daughters. If Jesus did it for them, He can certainly do it for us.

As we come to this final biblical table together:
What have you been thinking about since last week's feast?

Who did you live like a river toward and share what you learned at the feast last week?

How did that conversation go? How did your time together challenge you or confirm what you've been learning?

We are getting ready to pull up our chairs for Session Seven of this biblical feast. We are getting ready to *eat* the biblical meal prepared for us by our Father. He feeds. We receive. The Jewish people read the Scriptures over and over again. In the same way we don't eat one meal and then never eat again, we *eat* the Scriptures over and over again. We will never master them or get our hands around them fully. They are God-breathed, living and active. Speaking of the Scriptures, we find this quote in *Pirkei Avot* or *Ethics of the Fathers*,

> "Pore over [the Bible] again and again,
> for everything is contained in it;
> look into it,
> grow old and gray over it,
> and do not depart from it,
> for there is no better pursuit for you than this."[1]
> Rabbi Ben Bag Bag
> *Pirkei Avot 5:22* (first to second century AD)

Sit back. Breathe deep. Enjoy the feast!

THE FEAST

Use the following notes and space provided during our feast teaching time. Feel free to add your own notes as you watch.

The Greeks loved knowledge. The Romans loved power. The Jewish people have always loved the light. The Jewish people pore over the Scriptures again and again. Study is one of the highest forms of worship in Judaism. When you finish the Scriptures, you start over again. The Scriptures meet us right where we are every single time.

Jesus meets us right where we are, but He never leaves us there.

Notice the movement in these stories. No woman was even remotely the same after her interaction with Jesus.

Jesus did not come to turn things upside down. He came to turn things right side up—over and over again. And He's still doing it today!

Jesus met the Samaritan woman at Jacob's well. He met the woman as she sat against a wall at a meal. Jesus told stories and parables that included women, even teaching one parable where a lowly widow upended an unjust judge with her persistence. The woman caught in adultery was brought to him on the Southern Steps at the temple in Jerusalem with *everyone* looking on.

The Samaritan woman left the well and was never the same. She became the missionary for her entire village—telling them she had met the Messiah. The woman was pulled off the wall, generously lifted up, and sent away in peace. With Jesus, it was important to include women in the story. With Jesus, widows could upend unjust judges with their persistence.

GOD MEETS US WHERE WE ARE, BUT HE NEVER LEAVES US THERE.

Over and over in the Bible, we see God meeting people right where they were but never leaving them there. When God intervenes in a human life, there is change, transformation, and an invitation to journey together through life. We see God acting in this way in both Marys' stories this week. Young Mary was minding her own business when the angel showed up and announced she would birth the Messiah. Her life was never the same. Our other Mary, if she was the one against the wall in Luke 7, met Jesus when sitting against the wall and would eventually become Jesus' friend and ultimately a *talmid* (disciple) who sat at His feet.

Jesus meets us where we are, and He takes us somewhere. He faithfully shepherds us to the very end of our lives.

The woman caught in adultery was covered, generously lifted up, and sent away with the command to turn from sin and back to *shalom*.

> The Middle East, both then and now, has three primary cultural norms:
> ▣ Honor/Shame
> ▣ Hospitality
> ▣ Communal (we, not me)[2]

When the Lord is dealing out kingdom adventures, some of them are coming to girls, to women, to us!

One of the hardest yeses in the Bible belonged to a young girl—Mary (Miriam). In Jesus' day, young premenstrual girls were betrothed to eighteen-year-old boys. twelve-year-olds were marrying eighteen-year-olds. Betrothal usually lasted for one year.[3] We can imagine Mary as eleven or twelve years old when Gabriel visited her. She was betrothed, not yet married. She was probably premenstrual.[4] The adventure of birthing and being the mother of the Messiah came to a young girl. She had no idea what it would cost her. She knew it could cost her very life in an honor/shame culture. This might give insight as to why she "hurried" from Galilee all the way down to Judea.

One of the most unique yeses in the Bible belonged to another Mary (Miriam)—Mary the sister of Lazarus and Martha. She very well might have been the woman against the wall in our Luke 7 story. She might have been the one to bring the alabaster jar and tear jar to Simon's home.

> Now a man named Lazarus was sick. He was from Bethany, the village of Mary and her sister Martha. (This Mary, whose brother Lazarus now lay sick, was the same one who poured perfume on the Lord and wiped his feet with her hair.)
> JOHN 11:1-2

If she *is* the same woman, we see how far Jesus can take a person—from a low cultural place to Jesus' close friend!

Two Jewish Idioms within Discipleship in the First Century:
"Walking in the dust"[5]
"Sitting at the feet"[6]

"Let your house be a meeting place for the rabbis, and cover yourself in the dust of their feet, and drink in their words thirstily."[7]
—Attributed to Yose ben Yoezer,
   (second century BC)

When a rabbi came to your house, he would teach. He would sit (a posture of authority in Judaism), and his disciples would sit around him.

The disciple (*talmid*) relationship with a rabbi was very important in the first-century world of Jesus.

Talmidim didn't just want to know what their rabbi knew—they wanted to be like him. A disciple followed so closely to the rabbi that the dust of his feet got on him or her. A disciple didn't want any of the rabbi's words to "fall to the ground."

"Sitting at the feet" of a rabbi was a formal term in the first century. Recognized disciples (*talmidim*) "sat at the feet" of their rabbis. Remember, Paul "sat at the feet" of Gamaliel, the grandson of the infamous Hillel (Acts 22:3). This means he was a formal disciple of Gamaliel.

In Luke 10, Jesus was visiting Lazarus, Martha, and Mary. He started teaching. Mary "sat at the Lord's feet" (v. 39) learning, asking questions, interacting with the others. This passage seems to imply that Jesus had female followers.

What is your gaze fixed on?
most unique? most difficult?
Mary's actual name is Miriam

LET'S YESHIVA!

Each week we're going to take some time to *yeshiva*—to emulate the Middle Eastern communal way of discussing spiritual concepts and growing together in grace, as a biblical community. Discuss the following questions with your group.

What did you just *hear* or *see* in our feast together that you want to remember?

What one thing that we learned in our feast would you want to share with others this week?

How has Jesus brought *mishpat* (justice) and *tzedakah* (righteousness) into your life this week?

What has been one of the hardest yeses you have ever given to the Lord? Describe the situation.

What has been one of the most unique yeses you have ever given to the Lord? Describe the situation.

Is the Lord bringing an adventure to you right now in this season of your life? (I think He is bringing adventures into each of our lives.) What is it?

MARY–MIRIAM

This week's feast focused on two women, both named Mary. I like to call this week's teaching, "The Tale of Two Marys." However, Mary is not a Jewish name. Mary is the anglicized version of the Hebraic name Miriam.

The Jewish people are a deeply historical people. As a people, they intentionally remember, look back at their history as a people and what God has done for them, and take courage to live forward. Children were often named after the "greats" in Israel's history. Both Marys in our stories today, both Miriams, were named after the Miriam of the Old Testament—the sister of Moses and Aaron. [8]

Miriam was born to Amram and Jochebed during the Hebrews' enslavement to the Egyptians. She was born before Aaron and Moses. [9] The name Miriam means "bitterness," [10] a sentiment that illustrated life under Egyptian rule and oppression. [11] We see Miriam acting in great faith when she followed Moses in the basket as it made its way down the Nile River. When Pharaoh's daughter found him, Miriam approached her and offered a Jewish wet nurse to care for baby Moses. Pharaoh's daughter said *yes*, and Miriam went and got Jochebed, Moses' mother (Ex. 2).

Later, Miriam came to be known as a prophetess among the Israelites (Ex. 15:20).

READ EXODUS 15.

Moses and Miriam's song is recorded in Exodus 15 after the miraculous crossing of the Red Sea. She was a faithful daughter and sister in a season of peril and deliverance for the Israelites. She was a prophetess to her people—a prophetess with powerful words.

What Jewish girl wouldn't want to be named after such an incredible woman in Jewish history?

> Take a moment to consider the type of life you're leading. Is it marked by courage and trust in God? Or more trust in yourself? What do you want to be known for at the end of your life? Record your thoughts below or in a journal.

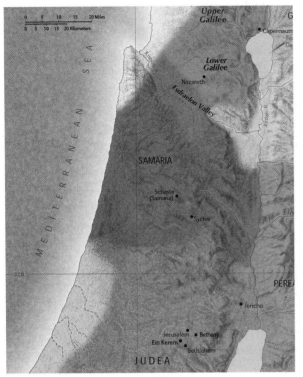

KINGDOM ADVENTURES

"I am the Lord's servant," Mary answered, "May your word to me be fulfilled." Then the angel left her. At that time Mary got ready and hurried to a town in the hill country of Judea, where she entered Zechariah's home and greeted Elizabeth.

LUKE 1:38-40

We wonder how many people in Nazareth would've believed Mary when they heard this story, if any at all. Even Joseph didn't believe her at first. He was preparing to "divorce her quietly" when an angel visited him in a dream to tell him it was true (Matt. 1:19-25). If Joseph had trouble getting his head and heart around this news, it's easy to imagine the greater community and village not being able to get their heads or hearts around it at all.

A betrothed, not-yet-married girl showed up pregnant? Mary lived in an honor/shame culture where women were stoned for such things. Mary "got ready and hurried" (v. 39). How far did she go? Not down the street. Not over two villages. She traveled all the way from the northern district of Galilee to the southern district of Judea. She went to Elizabeth's home, the home of her cousin.

Tradition places the home of Zechariah and Elizabeth in a tiny village called Ein Kerem, a village just southwest of historical Jerusalem. Ein Kerem means "spring of the vineyard." It is also the traditional site for the birth of John the Baptist. Because of this, there are many churches and monasteries in the area today.[12] The modern neighborhood (now a section of the ever-expanding Jerusalem) has a population of around two thousand people. Around three million visitors and pilgrims visit it each year.[13]

It's more than an eighty-mile journey from Nazareth to Ein Kerem. Mary was of the peasant class. She probably didn't ride a donkey those eighty miles. Instead, we can imagine her walking within a caravan of fellow travelers as they made their way south to Jerusalem. We imagine her walking those eighty miles, pregnant, with the Son of the Living God growing in her womb.

Mary, as a young betrothed girl, was minding her own business one day when Gabriel showed up out of nowhere and invited her into the adventure of a lifetime. She had no idea what it would cost her, but she knew it could cost her life. She also knew she and Jesus would probably always live with some kind of social stigma as to His legitimacy and the true story behind her pregnancy. We are forever grateful she said yes to the adventure that came to her.

> "Let us go on and take the adventure that shall fall to us."[14]
> —C. S. Lewis, *The Lion, the Witch and the Wardrobe*

When the Living God wants to hand out kingdom adventures, some of them are coming to girls, to women, to us! We don't need to go find kingdom adventures—they have a way of finding us.

Think of all the times you were minding your own business and something came out of nowhere and grabbed your heart—something that changed the direction of your life. How has it shaped you? Changed you? Matured you? What has it cost you?

If God were to approach you with a new kingdom adventure today, is there anything that would keep you from saying yes to Him? Explain.

CARAVAN

In antiquity, you never traveled alone. Traveling alone was considered dangerous. Think of the story of the good Samaritan—the man traveling alone was mugged and beaten.

In the communal ancient Near Eastern culture, people traveled together in caravans—individuals and families would set out on a journey together. Such a partnership provided a collective sense of protection, companionship, and shared resources along the journey. It also strengthened relationships as they went along.

We imagine Mary traveling from Nazareth to Ein Kerem with a caravan. She probably knew some of the people she was traveling with, maybe most of them.

I sometimes wonder if Mary told anyone about the angel visiting her and what he had said. I wonder if she told anyone in that ancient caravan that she was carrying the Christ child in her womb.

CHOOSING WHAT IS BETTER

As Jesus and his disciples were on their way, he came to a village where a woman named Martha opened her home to him. She had a sister called Mary, who sat at the Lord's feet listening to what he said. But Martha was distracted by all the preparations that had to be made. She came to him and asked, "Lord, don't you care that my sister has left me to do the work by myself? Tell her to help me!" "Martha, Martha," the Lord answered, "you are worried and upset about many things, but few things are needed—or indeed only one. Mary has chosen what is better, and it will not be taken from her."

LUKE 10:38-42

 Look at this Bible passage through the **Western lens**, the framework of understanding first and allowing that understanding to fuel belief. Write down what you notice in this story.

 Look at this Bible passage through the **Middle Eastern lens**, the framework of believing first and allowing that belief to fuel understanding. Write down what you notice in this story.

Mary sat at the feet of Jesus, listening and learning as He taught His disciples. *If you wait to understand everything about this passage to believe it, you might never move forward. If you take the Word as is and let it settle in your heart, you will begin to move forward with new perspective, fresh insight, and quickened living, among other things.*

 Look at this Bible passage through the **Western lens,** asking the question, "What does this teach me about *me*?" Write down what you notice in this story.

 Look at this Bible passage through the **Middle Eastern lens,** asking the question, "What does this teach me about *God*?" Write down what you notice in this story.

 Look at this Bible passage through the **Middle Eastern lens,** asking the question, "What does this teach me about *Jesus*?" Write down what you notice in this story.

Which perspective encourages you more, generously lifts you up more? Explain.

WALKING FORWARD

We have come to the end of our seven-week feast together. Much has been taught and shared in the teaching times. Much has been taught and shared in our times of *yeshiva*. We've been learning to take off our Western lenses and put on our Middle Eastern lenses when we read and eat the Bible. We've been learning that Jesus is *better* than we ever knew!

We've spent seven weeks learning to stare at God and glance at our lives. We've been learning to posture ourselves to receive, to be fed the Word of God by our Father. We've been living like rivers and not lakes, giving what we've been getting in our times together in the Scriptures to others. The Spirit of God takes the Word and feeds the woman of God for the work of God. The Scriptures are living and active—we are living too. God-breathed life in the Word has been meeting our Spirit-quickened hearts, and we are better for having spent these seven weeks together.

We've been getting to know Jesus in His Jewish, first-century world. We've also been getting to know woman in her Jewish, first-century world. We've watched Jesus relate to a diverse grouping of women (Samaritan, Jewish, widow, adulteress) time and again with a unified sense of posture and purpose. Jesus moved toward them; He was for them and with them. He was working toward a deep and an ancient restoration as He brought *mishpat* (justice) and *tzedakah* (righteousness)— a generous lifting up to each one. Jesus' love is kind, fierce, unprecedented, and epic.

Jesus did not come to turn things upside down. He came to turn things right side up. The goal of every rabbi was to teach his disciples (*talmidim*) how to *halakh* (walk) the *halakha* (way or path) of God—the path of *shalom*. Jesus intended for women everywhere to live generously lifted up. If He did it for them, He can certainly do it for us today.

> The question now is—How do you want to *halakh* (walk) forward after this seven-week feast? What do you want to remember forever? What are you committed to keep sharing with others?

Write down your main takeaways from this seven-week feast.

Write down your main commitments in the way you *halakh* (walk) forward with your life.

How do you want to live differently after sharing in this seven-week feast?

What would it look like for you to live more intentionally as one who is being generously lifted up by Jesus each and every day?

WRAP-UP

CELEBRATION

CELEBRATION

After you've finished all of Session Seven, take a few moments to remember and celebrate what God has done in your life. Feel free to call or text your small group friends so you can praise God together for what He's done.

In the West, we don't always know how to end something. But I say we should end in celebration. As a people who believe God is in the business of restoring the world to peace with Him, followers of Jesus Christ should be a people of celebration. The way we celebrate shows what we think about God.

In the Hebrew culture, they practice two fundamental spiritual rhythms (among others)—remembering and celebrating. These spiritual rhythms have changed my life. We've already talked about *zakhar*, remembering, a bit. But we've yet to discuss celebration as a spiritual rhythm.

I believe God put these spiritual practices before His people because He knows that we are a forgetful people. We tend to most easily forget the faithfulness of the Lord in our lives, because life kicks us all in the gut. The pain of the immediate can make it harder to remember what He has done and the promise of what He will do for us. These rhythms of remembering and celebrating anchor us in reality. We need them because so often how we're feeling isn't faithful to the truth of who God is. Remembering takes us back to the actual historical record of who God is and how He has not failed us yet, nor will He ever fail us.

There's something about remembering in a way of active celebration that moves us forward—encouraged, emboldened, and courageous enough to lean into the thing in front of us. We think of memory as just looking back, but for the Hebrew people, it's a looking back to look forward. When we remember God's faithful record, both in our lives and in the family of God past and present, it quickens a sense of celebration in us because it reminds us of the eternal over the temporal. It reminds us of resurrection swallowing death. It reminds us God is going to see the story all the way through, shepherding us and this whole crazy world back to *shalom*.

We're going to live forever, in perfect *shalom* with God. Celebration connects us to the everyday reality that a deep and ancient restoration and renewal of all things is happening, even now in the midst of the mundane.

Pausing to reconnect with the meta-narrative of the Bible moves us forward. It quickens us to think again and anew; if this is who God is, then who do I want to be? So let's take a few minutes to consider, remember, celebrate, and move forward, eager to witness God's restoration in us and around us. Remembering and celebrating are some of the ways we take heart as daughters. Remember who God is; root your courage in His faithful character. Celebrate His love for you.

What could these rhythms of remembering and celebrating look like in your life? In your personal time with God? In your family or community of faith?

In light of everything we have learned about Jesus, who do you want to be? How do you want to live your life? Differently from how you were before this? Explain your thoughts.

How can you become a creature who remembers and celebrates God's goodness to you?

Below, or in your journal, take a few minutes to practice these spiritual rhythms.
Remember—record a few ways you've seen God be faithful in your life or in the life of the children of God.

Celebrate—how do those things you recalled above fuel you to rejoice in Him and live forward?

LEADER GUIDE

LEADER GUIDE INTRODUCTION

Jesus and Women is a video- and discussion-based Bible study. The weekly personal study along with the feast teaching videos will promote honest conversation as you study Scripture together. Since conversation is essential to the experience, you'll find a few starter questions in both the *Discuss* section and the leader guide to help get the discussion rolling.

This study may be used in a variety of large or small group settings including churches, homes, offices, coffee shops, or other desirable locations.

TIPS ON LEADING THIS BIBLE STUDY

PRAY: As you prepare to lead *Jesus and Women,* remember that prayer is essential. Set aside time each week to pray for the women in your group. Listen to their needs and the struggles they're facing, so you can bring them before the Lord. Though organizing and planning are important, protect your time of prayer before each gathering. Encourage your women to include prayer as part of their own daily spiritual disciplines as well.

GUIDE: Accept women where they are, but also set expectations that motivate commitment. Be consistent and trustworthy. Encourage women

to follow through on the study, attend the group sessions, and engage with the personal study. Listen carefully, responsibly guide discussion, and keep confidences shared within the group. Be honest and vulnerable by sharing what God is teaching you throughout the study. Most women will follow your lead and be more willing to share and participate when they see your transparency. Reach out to women of different ages, backgrounds, and stages of life. This variety of experience is sure to make your conversation and time together richer.

CONNECT: Stay engaged with the women in your group. Use social media, emails, text messages, phone calls, or a quick note in the mail to connect with them and share prayer needs throughout the week. Let them know when you are praying specifically for them. Root everything in Scripture and encourage women in their relationships with Jesus.

CELEBRATE: Leave time at the end of your Session Seven group meeting to celebrate what God has done by having your group share what they've learned and how they've grown. Pray together about what further steps God may be asking them to take as a result of this study.

TIPS ON ORGANIZING THIS BIBLE STUDY

TALK TO YOUR PASTOR OR MINISTER OF EDUCATION OR DISCIPLESHIP: If you're leading this as part of a local church, ask for your leaders' input, prayers, and support.

SECURE YOUR LOCATION: Think about the number of women you can accommodate in the designated location. Reserve tables, chairs, or media equipment for the videos, music, and additional audio needs.

PROVIDE CHILDCARE: If you are targeting moms of young children and/or single moms, childcare will be essential.

PROVIDE RESOURCES: Order the needed number of Bible study books. You might buy a few extra for last minute sign-ups. The teaching videos are available via redemption code printed on the card in the back of each Bible study book.

PLAN AND PREPARE: Become familiar with the Bible study resource and leader helps available. Preview the video session and prepare the outline you will follow to lead the group meeting. Go to *lifeway.com/jesusandwomen* to find free extra leader helps and promotional resources for your study.

EVALUATE

At the end of each group session, ask yourself: What went well? What could be improved? Did you see women's lives transformed? Did your group grow closer to Christ and to one another?

NEXT STEPS

Even after the study concludes, follow up and challenge women to stay involved through another Bible study, church opportunity, or ministry that will continue their spiritual growth and encourage friendships. Provide several options of ministry opportunities members can participate in individually or as a group to apply what they have learned through this study.

SESSION ONE

1. Welcome women to the study, and distribute Bible study books.

2. Watch the Session One video, using the *Watch* summary and notes pages (pp. 13–15) as you come to the weekly feast.

3. Following the video, lead women through the *Yeshiva* group discussion questions (p. 16).

4. Remind the group members to complete the personal study on pages 17–27 at home on their own this week before you meet again.

5. Close the session with prayer.

SESSION TWO

1. Welcome the women to Session Two of *Jesus and Women*.

2. Watch the Session Two video, using the *Watch* summary and notes pages (pp. 32–35), and encourage the women to take notes as Kristi teaches.

3. Following the video, lead women through the *Yeshiva* group discussion questions (p. 36).

4. Remind the group members to complete the personal study on pages 37–45 at home on their own this week before you meet again.

5. Close: Spend time together praying for God to heal any places where the women in your group have been oppressed or treated badly. Ask for God to bring restoration in those areas. Consider giving women the opportunity to share, and then gather around and pray for each one specifically.

SESSION THREE

1. Welcome the women to Session Three of *Jesus and Women*.

2. Watch the Session Three video, using the *Watch* summary and notes pages (pp. 50–53), and encourage the women to take notes as Kristi teaches.

3. Following the video, lead women through the *Yeshiva* group discussion questions (p. 54).

4. Remind the group members to complete the personal study on pages 55–63 at home on their own this week before you meet again.

5. Close: Ask women to form groups of two to four people and share how shame has paralyzed them in the past or is currently paralyzing them. Instruct them to pray for each other after they've shared.

SESSION FOUR

1. Welcome the women to Session Four of *Jesus and Women*.

2. Watch the Session Four video, using the *Watch* summary and notes pages (pp. 68–71), and encourage the women to take notes as Kristi teaches.

3. Following the video, lead women through the *Yeshiva* group discussion questions (p. 72).

4. Remind the group members to complete the personal study on pages 73–81 at home on their own this week before you meet again.

5. Close: Remind women that knowing who Jesus truly is, is critical to knowing what's really true. And to know Him you have to spend time with Him in prayer and in His Word. Challenge your group to make time with Jesus a priority this week.

SESSION FIVE

1. Welcome the women to Session Five of *Jesus and Women*.

2. Watch the Session Five video, using the *Watch* summary and notes pages (pp. 86–89), and encourage the women to take notes as Kristi teaches.

3. Following the video, lead women through the *Yeshiva* group discussion questions (p. 90).

4. Remind the group members to complete the personal study on pages 91–99 at home on their own this week before you meet again.

5. Close: Split up into smaller groups and ask the second to last *Yeshiva* question: If Jesus were to be amazed at you right now, would it be for your faith or lack of faith? What circumstances are challenging your faith right now? What situations are encouraging your faith right now? Instruct the women to pray for one another after they have shared.

SESSION SIX

1. Welcome the women to Session Six of *Jesus and Women*.

2. Watch the Session Six video, using the *Watch* summary and notes pages (pp. 104–107), and encourage the women to take notes as Kristi teaches.

3. Following the video, lead women through the *Yeshiva* group discussion questions (p. 108).

4. Remind the group members to complete the personal study on pages 109–117 at home on their own this week before you meet again.

5. Close: Ask women to relate the story of one woman they have been "living like a river" toward and with whom they have been sharing what they have been learning in our feasts. Lead women to pair up and pray for those individuals they've been sharing with. Ask God to be near to that person. Pray for that person to know God intimately as Savior and Lord.

SESSION SEVEN

1. Welcome the women to Session Seven of *Jesus and Women*.

2. Watch the Session Seven video, using the *Watch* summary and notes pages (pp. 122–125), and encourage the women to take notes as Kristi teaches.

3. Following the video, lead women through the *Yeshiva* group discussion questions (p. 126).

4. Remind the group members to complete the personal study on pages 127–133.

5. Close: Direct women to share what is hindering their trust in the Lord—what might be keeping them from saying yes to God. Lead in a prayer thanking God

GLOSSARY

Ben Sira/Sirach (Person): Originally from Jerusalem, Joshua son of Sira (or Yeshua Ben Sira) was a scribe who started a Jewish school in, presumably, Alexandria, Egypt, around 200 BC. Ben Sira was very knowledgeable of both Scripture (what he considered Scripture is now known as our Old Testament) and the human condition. However, his teachings were characterized by harsh treatment of both slaves and women; he considered them mere possessions to be handled however one wanted. These teachings were difficult to fathom in his day and are even more so in our own.[1]

The Book of Ben Sira/Sirach: Though numerous titles exist for this book of wisdom literature composed in the second century BC, it's most commonly known as *Ecclesiasticus* or *Sirach*. Ben Sira wrote the text in Hebrew originally, and decades later his grandson translated it to Greek. Though not considered canon by Protestants, both Catholic and Orthodox traditions deem it Scripture and include it in their list of Deuterocanonical works or Apocrypha. In content, it's most akin to the genre of wisdom literature as it contains numerous proverbs and ethical teachings.[2]

Cultural Considerations: As we approach the Bible with a new Middle Eastern lens, it's important to understand some significant differences between our culture today and the cultures of the first-century world. Though our cultural heritage and worldviews are valid, we in the 21st century approach the Bible in three vastly different ways than people two thousand years ago would have approached the Scripture.

First, we live in an innocent/guilt culture. This carries significance in the way we process sin as well as how we implement justice. (We know the drill: "Innocent until proven guilty," and "Let your conscience be your guide.") What happens, however, when justice cannot be found? Or when justice is faulty? To what point do we trust our consciences when we've seared them to such a degree that we no longer feel guilty when we do something wrong?

In the Middle East they view the world differently. They function on an honor/shame continuum. In this culture, because everything centered on the family—religion, rituals, and politics—every member of that family carries the responsibility of bringing honor to his or her relatives. Shame is a reproach, and it comes in many forms. For example, cheating another family in a business transaction, being barren, and maintaining inappropriate relationships all bring shame on the rest of the family. On the other hand, fulfilling one's role as a daughter or son, wife or husband, priest or ruler brings honor. As a member of a family unit, everything one does either brings honor or shame, and in regards to sin and justice, all of it is connected to honor and shame.

This leads us to our second significant cultural difference. We emphasize the individual, but Middle Easterners two thousand years ago were all about the community. Notice how crucial this is to our understanding of the cultural difference we just discussed—innocence/guilt and honor/shame. In an individualistic culture like ours, sin is a private matter, lodged inside of us, and, therefore, sin is somewhat relative. What might be a sin for you, may not be for me; my weaknesses and strengths are different than yours. In a communal culture, however, everyone understands what is expected, and few things are done in secret. Even David, when he took in Bathsheba, was warned by his servants of who she was—someone else's wife! When living in community, sin is worn on the sleeve. Everyone knows what is happening, and a person's actions either bring shame or honor to his or her community.

Last, ancient (and present) Middle Eastern culture is highly hospitable, and I'm not just talking about having people over for some afternoon tea on the front porch. Hospitality was and is considered one of the greatest virtues one can express. If a stranger comes up to your house, or is simply walking nearby, you must invite them in. And when you do invite them in, your guests receive nothing but your absolute best! If you've been planning a special birthday party for a child, that visitor gets the party. If you've been saving for that new car, a large percentage of those savings goes to the guest in the form of food and entertainment. In certain nomadic cultures today, a family is required by custom and tradition to offer you their best food and drink for three days. It does not matter if you are Jewish, Muslim, Christian, Hindu, or Taoist. If you pass by or seek shelter in their dwelling, they will care for you as an honored guest.

Cultural Idioms: Within any language, we find nuance and cultural understanding that many times cannot be grasped by the simple definition of individual words within a phrase. If I say, "I'm in hot water," I'm not communicating I'm sitting in boiling water. Instead, I simply mean I'm in trouble. Other examples include: "They let the cat out of the bag," "It's raining cats and dogs," and "Break a leg." We have similar phrases in the Bible. But because we don't know the language and culture well, we often lose these phrases in translation or interpretive reading. For example, in the context of the Bible, having a "good eye" means being generous;[3] "to hear" means to literally hear but also to obey;[4] and "stiff-necked" means stubborn.[5] Some idioms have carried over to us in English, but there are many that remain unclear even to translators.

Davar: In English, one meaning of *davar* is "word." In this case, Hebrew speakers use the same noun as a verb too, so *davar* means not only "word," but also "he speaks." In fact, one of the many things that makes the Hebrew language of the Old Testament so fascinating is that words can carry multiple meanings—even in the same verse or phrase. For example, *davar* can also be translated as "thing."[6]

Because of this close connection between words and objects, religious Jews in the ancient world chose their words very carefully. (This is still true today.) They rarely, if ever, gossip. They call it "an evil tongue." Why? Because words carry weight. What and how we speak of ourselves and others matters. For example: "And God said ... And there was .... " In Genesis 1 God speaks a word, and that word becomes a thing.

Hagah: *Hagah* is the Hebrew word that describes the sound of a lion roaring over its caught prey. In fact, like many Hebrew words, *hagah* is an onomatopoeia—it sounds like what it describes. Funny, then, that of several words available to the author of Psalm 1, he decided upon *hagah* to describe a way of poring over God's Torah. Most translators use the word "meditate" as the best choice. Unfortunately, when we think of "meditate," many of us envision a monk with legs crossed on a lonely mountain. For the author of Psalm 1:2, however, the vision of studying God's Word day and night is more like a lion roaring over its prey. You're so hungry, and you cannot get enough![7]

Ha-man/Manhue: Translated today as "manna," *ha-man* (also transliterated as *manhue*) originally was a question the Israelites asked when they first saw a flakey substance like frost covering the ground. They said, "*Manhue*?" "What is it?" And so, *ha-man* is how it came to be called. God provided this substance for the Israelites every single day during their forty years in the wilderness, and this remembered provision came to be known as "daily bread" by the first century.[8]

Haver (pl. Haverim): Literally meaning "friend" or "companion," *haver* in the first century was a study partner and fellow disciple—someone you could ask hard questions of and expect hard questions from in return. *Haverim* pushed each other, sometimes to the brink, in order to get to the truth. Calling someone your *haver* also implied that he or she followed Torah in a similar fashion as you, maybe even following the same rabbi. You would spend the majority of your days with these *haverim* discussing what was most important in your life and the lives of those around you.[9]

Kanaf (pl. Kanafayim): *Kanaf* in English means "corner." When God commanded the Israelites to wear tassels, He instructed the people to place these tassels on the corners of their garments. *Kanaf* also translates as "wing," as we see in Isaiah 6:2 where the seraphim each having six wings.[10]

L'chaim: A traditional Hebrew toast similar to "Cheers!" in English, *L'chaim* simply means "to life!"[11]

Mayim Chayim: Because ritual purification was of paramount importance for Jews in the first century, strategies to keep oneself pure were a significant topic of conversation. As part of that important conversation, the sages discussed the kind of water that was appropriate, not only for purity laws but also for basic hygiene and living. *Mayim chayim* means "living water," and it refers to water that remains moving, not stagnant. Sources for living water include rain, springs, wells, streams, rivers, and freshwater lakes. Basically, any water source that is not carried by human hands or stored in cisterns but comes directly from God Himself is considered *mayim chayim*.[12]

This imagery shows up all over the Old Testament as an image for God, and especially in the New Testament Book of John. Jesus speaks of living water both in John 4 and John 7, where He metaphorically speaks of the Holy Spirit. We see, then, that living water served not only a ritualistic and hygienic purpose, but also a religious and metaphorical purpose. For a people who find themselves in the desert more often than not, few things are more precious or more powerful than the imagery and actuality of *mayim chayim*, living water!

Mikveh (pl. Mikve'ot): Beginning in earnest in the first century BC and proceeding to this day, ritual purification (or *mikveh*) has served many purposes throughout the centuries. The forebearer of Christian baptism, *mikve'ot* were stepped immersion pools.[13] An individual would enter the *mikveh* naked, fully submerge him or herself, and upon exiting the waters be rendered ritually pure. At least two witnesses had to be present to confirm full immersion.[14] (Because of the emphasis on modesty in Middle Eastern culture, men and women would submerge themselves separately.) The archaeological evidence shows hundreds of these pools. The ruins of these pools serve as a defacto map showing the extent of first century BC and AD Jewish populations and influence—especially in the modern-day states of Israel and Jordan.[15]

Mishnah: When God gave His Torah to Moses at Mount Sinai, Jews believe He also gave a second set of laws called *Mishnah*, "that which is repeated."[16] The written Torah (or *Mikra*) was far greater in importance, and the oral Torah (or *Mishnah*) expanded and explained what was meant in the written Torah. The *Mishnah* itself explains how it came into existence: "Moses received the Torah at Sinai and transmitted it to Joshua, Joshua to the elders, and the elders to the prophets, and the prophets to the men of the Great Assembly" (*Pirkei Avot 1:1*).[17] From the Great Assembly, that tradition of interpretation carried on through the sages of the first centuries BC and AD, many of whom are called rabbis ("my great ones").[18]

By the beginning of the third century AD it became necessary to write the traditions that had been handed down to that point, a project spearheaded by a man known as Yehudah ha-Nasi, or in English Judah the Prince.[19] This written document offers a small window into Judaism from as early as 300 BC to as late as approximately AD 200.[20] It's divided into six main sections and seven to twelve subsections, starting with the longest and ending with the shortest.[21] Interestingly, the early church organized Paul's letters in the same way in the Bible—longest to shortest.[22]

Mishpat: Translated most often as "justice" from the Hebrew, *mishpat* serves a special function in the economy of God. Since God advocates for the poor and the oppressed, especially widows and orphans, He expects His followers to do the same. At its core, *mishpat* isn't so much concerned with innocence and guilt as much as honor and shame. To bring justice to the world, God exalts the humble by raising their honor and covering their shame.

Tied closely to another word, *tzedakah*, *mishpat* deals with punishment for wrongdoing, but it is also concerned with equal rights for all—rich and poor, female and male, foreigner and native born. We see a good example of *mishpat* in Numbers 27:1-11 with a tribal land dispute involving a man named Zelophehad who had five daughters and no sons. Strictly because of their gender, the daughters were excluded from any inheritance, but once their case came before Moses, God granted their request and gave them land. This is how *mishpat* works: God raised the daughters' honor by treating them equally—even in a patriarchal society. Ultimately, *mishpat* concerns giving everyone what is due them, whether that is protection, provision, or punishment.[23]

Mount Gerizim: Second in height only to its neighbor Mount Ebal, Mount Gerizim serves as the most sacred location for Samaritans (who still live there to this day). In approximately 128 BC, Jews destroyed the Samaritan temple and attempted to force conversion on all people groups living in the land, including the Samaritans.[24] Needless to say, this attack enlivened the Samaritans to such a degree that animosity on both sides piqued in the first centuries BC and AD.

Mt. Gerizim overshadows the New Testament town of Sychar and specifically Jacob's well.[25] Because of its proximity, the site figures prominently in the conversations Jesus had with the Samaritan woman in John 4.[26]

Parashah (pl. Parashot): Because the Torah held the primary place within all of Scripture, after the exile, Jews decided to have all five books read aloud throughout the course of a year. In order to accomplish this, they divided the Torah into fifty-four *parashot*, or sections, allowing for one section of a book to be read at the same time every year. Thus, every week a new section of Scripture was studied all week and read aloud in the synagogue for Sabbath.

Literary evidence for this practice occurs not only in the Dead Sea Scrolls, but also in the New Testament. In Luke 4 Jesus follows up the Torah reading with a passage from Isaiah, and in Acts 15, the Jerusalem Council mentions how the Torah was being read in the synagogues every single week.[27]

Rabbi Eliezer: Living at the turn of the first and second centuries AD, Rabbi Eliezer is one of the most quoted sages in the *Mishnah*. He unfortunately made a name for himself through his disagreements with his fellow sages and his more conservative approach to Scripture, eventually being expelled from the Sanhedrin because of a view regarding the usability of a specific kind of oven.[28]

Schools of Hillel and Shammai: Though very diverse, Pharisaic Judaism in the first centuries BC and AD was ultimately held together and led by two men, Rabbi Hillel[29] and Rabbi Shammai,[30] along with their disciples. Both centered in Jerusalem. Hillel, who lived from approximately 110 BC to AD 10, took a more generous and lenient approach to Scripture. On the other hand, Shammai, who lived from approximately 50 BC to AD 30 took a far more conservative and stern view.

To highlight their differences, a story is told about a student who desired to learn Torah while standing on one foot. When he went to Shammai to inquire how to do this, Shammai beat him with a stick and drove him away, inferring rather violently that it takes a lifetime to master Torah, and it is prideful and insolent to believe one could memorize it while standing on one foot. When the young man went to Hillel and asked the same question, Hillel replied, "What is hateful to you, don't do to others. This is the whole of Torah; the rest is the explanation. Now, go and learn it" (*Shabbat 31a*).[31]

Known for how they disagreed with one another, they were almost always shown in rabbinic literature together, but with opposing arguments. Their differences centered on how to interpret Torah for the culture in which they lived. For example, the question arose as to how one should light the candles for Hanukkah; should you light all eight the first night and subsequently light one less candle for each remaining night? Or should you light one the first night and add to it for the remaining nights? Shammai said the light slowly dwindles through the holiday, while Hillel said it grew (*Shabbat 21b:5*).[32] It was decided, as was the case in most matters, that Hillel's view was followed and not Shammai's. Amazingly, Jesus entered into their debates as well, and in every argument (with the exception of divorce) Jesus favored Hillel's interpretation as opposed to Shammai's.[33]

Septuagint: A Greek translation of the Hebrew Bible. Greek speaking Jews used the Septuagint (often abbreviated "LXX") as their main text. The early Christians used this translation primarily, which is why Paul quotes from it so often. The history of how the Jewish people came to have this translation is shrouded in myth and mystery, but scholars date the translation to the third to second century BC when a ruler named Ptolemy II invited seventy-two Jewish scholars to Egypt.[34] The story goes that upon arrival, these seventy-two Jewish leaders were placed in seventy-two rooms in which they were individually asked to translate the Hebrew Scriptures into Greek, in order that future Greek-speaking generations wouldn't lose the Word of God. Hence, the Latin word for "seventy," Septuagint.[35]

Tallit: Used to cover the head during prayer, the *tallit* is best translated as a prayer shawl. *Tallits* come in different sizes and colors, but they traditionally extend to arm's length on both sides and can be wrapped around a person like a shawl. Significantly, the corners of the *tallit* represent wings, and symbolically the wings of God serve as a covering for the one praying.[36]

Talmud (Jerusalem and Babylonian): After the *Mishnah* was written down at the beginning of the third century AD, over the next few hundred years, scribes and teachers contributed further commentaries on the written text. That collection of work came to be known as the *Gemara*. As two large centers of learning developed within Judaism—one in Galilee and one in Babylon—these two academies put together the *Mishnah* and *Gemara* into one work known as the *Talmud*. The school in Galilee (Tiberias, specifically) was known as the *Jerusalem Talmud*, while the school in Babylon became known as the *Babylonian Talmud*. Composed in the fourth and fifth centuries AD, respectively, the *Babylonian Talmud* became the more authoritative work.

Perhaps the simplest way to think of these Jewish works is to understand that the Torah is central and most important in all matters of life. The *Mishnah* functions somewhat as a commentary on the Torah, and the *Talmud* serves as a commentary on the *Mishnah*. If a person were to venture off into a school (*yeshiva*) today, he or she would discover that not only are students studying and memorizing the Torah, they are also studying and memorizing the *Talmud*.

A story is told about a recent scholar in Jerusalem who one day showed up with the entire *Babylonian Talmud* in hand. (Understand, this would be like carrying all the volumes of the *Encyclopedia Britannica* around with you.) Upon entering the classroom, he found one of his prize students and said, "I have committed this to memory. You now go and do the same."[37]

Tanakh (Hebrew Bible): What Christians call the Old Testament, Jews call the *Tanakh* or *Mikra* ("that which is called out/read"). Just as we Christians have subdivided the Old Testament into categories (for example, the Law, History, Poetry, Major Prophets, Minor Prophets), so too have the Jews. The letters T, N, and K come from the first letter of those three sections of Scripture for the Jew: Torah (Instruction or Law), *Nevi'im* (Prophets), and *Ketuvim* (Writings).[38]

The weight of authority given to these sections, however, is another matter. For the Jew, nothing is more important than Torah. The Torah is the first place they go when deriving authority from Scripture. The books of Torah include Genesis, Exodus, Leviticus, Numbers, and Deuteronomy, what scholars today call the Pentateuch ("five books"). Though traditionally translated as "law," the word Torah implies instruction more than law.[39] The Jewish people carry the idea that the commandments offer freedom more than oppression. The commandments are parameters that allow a person to function well in their family, tribe, and nation.

The second section, the Prophets, functions almost like a commentary on the Torah, offering interpretations and examples of what to do and what not to do within the system of laws God has set up. The books of the Hebrew Bible within this section include: Joshua, Judges, 1 and 2 Samuel, 1 and 2 Kings, Isaiah, Jeremiah, Ezekiel, Hosea, Joel, Amos, Obadiah, Jonah, Micah, Nahum, Habakkuk, Zephaniah, Haggai, Zechariah, and Malachi.

The third section, the Writings, is considered the least authoritative, but is still considered God's Word and part of the Bible. The books include: Psalms, Proverbs, Job, Song of Songs, Ruth, Lamentations, Ecclesiastes, Esther, Daniel, Ezra, Nehemiah, and 1 and 2 Chronicles.[40]

The books of the Hebrew Bible, though reckoned differently than ours and in a different order, offer the same content. In the Hebrew Bible, the books fall relatively in the order in which they were written. This leads us to a fascinating theological insight: The entirety of the Hebrew Bible begins and ends in a similar place. *Tanakh* starts with Genesis and finishes with Chronicles, theologically driving an exiled people back to Jerusalem and its environs—in essence, to a new Eden. Thus, what begins in Genesis in a garden (the garden of Eden), ends in Chronicles with a desire and call to return to a new "Eden," the land of Israel with Jerusalem as its epicenter.

Our order of books within the Old Testament also points to a new reality. God speaks, and physical existence comes to be; God's Word is made flesh. By ending our Old Testament with Malachi, we look with anticipation not to a place, but to a person. Thus, we see how God's Word was made flesh not only in the creation of the universe, but also in the bringing forth of the Son—Jesus—who was and is the perfect manifestation of God. "The Word became flesh and made His dwelling among us" (John 1:14).

Tekhelet: The **tekhelet** is the blue cord in each *tzitzit*. Because the memory of the precise dying process has been lost, Orthodox Jews today very rarely incorporate the blue dye in a tassel. Through archaeological discoveries, however, scholars have identified the Murex snail as the most likely producer of the blue color needed, and as further research takes place, perhaps the dying process will be reinstated.[41]

Tzedakah: *Tzedakah* means "righteousness" and so much more. Placed within the realm of relationships, *tzedakah* serves to make things right, and it does so through generosity. Another translation of the Hebrew word could easily be mercy.[42] In fact, an act of righteousness in the first century was giving to the poor. (See Matt. 6:1-4.) By not sharing with others, one violates the very justice, will, and command of God. This practice reveals that *tzedakah* is not optional in God's economy.

When coupled with *mishpat*, as is the case dozens of times in the Old Testament, we can clearly see the character of God Himself. We first see these words together in Genesis 18:19 when God says of Abraham: "For I have chosen him, so that he will direct his children and his household after him to keep the way of the Lord by doing what is *right* and *just*, so that the Lord will bring about for Abraham what he has promised him" (emphasis added). As evidenced in this passage, the way of the Lord is practicing both *mishpat* and *tzedakah* together—a generous lifting up.

Tzitzit (pl. tzitziyot): In Numbers 15:37-40 God commanded the Israelites to wear tassels on the corners of their garments. The *tzitzit* or tassel reminded the wearer of God's commandments in order that they might be obeyed.[43] So important was the passage of Scripture that to this day it is recited at the end of reciting the *Shema* in Jewish prayers. The significance of how and where the tassels were to be tied and worn grew just before and after the destruction of the temple, and Jesus, as a religious Jew, would have worn *tzitziyot* on His garments. Jesus actually referred to tassels in Matthew 23:5 in His criticism of hypocritical Pharisees who tried to make theirs extra long.

The Greek term used for tassels in the Old Testament is *kraspedon*, meaning corner or hem. It's the same Greek term used when the hemorrhaging woman grabbed the hem of Jesus' garment.[44]

Today, *tzitziyot* are carefully tied so that every knot and space carry meaning (in other words, five knots represent the five Books of Moses [Torah], and four spaces between the knots represent the four letters in God's sacred name).[45]

Yeshiva: Today, *yeshiva* is a formal term referring to an established educational system focused on studying the Torah and the *Talmud*. In the first century, however, the emphasis on the term lay in how a teacher interpreted a specific passage of Scripture or theological concept and if that teaching was valid. How would a community determine validity? *Yeshiva*.

Yeshiva occurred constantly as students would debate questions or comments from a teacher. They were "sitting in" the concept so to speak, arguing and debating among themselves whether or not what the teacher communicated should be implemented into daily life and how it could be done. Learning occurred in a multidimensional way as arguments among peers and teachers were raised and discussed. In this line of thinking, the better a community knows the Bible, the more profound the insights as other passages and teachers' interpretations are brought in to bear on the topic.[46]

Zakhar: Occurring more than 230 times in the Old Testament alone, *zakhar* means "remembered."[47] It appears more than 100 times in the positive form, "do not forget." When God speaks to His people, especially through prophets like Moses, remembrance is a repeated theme. One of the ways that Jews in the first century took God's words to heart was by repeating their lessons over and over again. In the *Babylonian Talmud* we read these words from Hillel (who lived in the first century BC): "One who reviews his studies one hundred times is not comparable to the one who reviews his studies one hundred and one times" (*Chagigah 9b*).[48] In other words, repetition solidifies learning and is key to remembrance.

ENDNOTES

Introduction

1. Russell Moore, "If you hate Jews, you hate Jesus," *The Washington Post*, Oct. 31, 2018, accessed Oct. 21, 2019, https://www.washingtonpost.com/religion/2018/10/29/christian-message-about-pittsburgh-synagogue-shooting-if-you-hate-jews-you-hate-jesus-too/.
2. Gary M. Burge, *Jesus, the Middle Eastern Storyteller* (Grand Rapids, MI: Zondervan, 2009), 11.

Session One

1. Merriam-Webster, s.v. "Yeshiva," accessed September 12, 2019, https://www.merriam-webster.com/dictionary/yeshiva.
2. Charlotte Elisheva Fonrobert, Martin S. Jaffee, eds., *The Cambridge Companion to the Talmud and Rabbinic Literature*, (New York: Cambridge University Press, 2007, 58).
3. Rabbi Yissachar Dov Rubin, *Talelei Oros—The Holiday Anthology* (Jerusalem: Feldheim Publishers, 2003), 207.
4. John D. Garr, Life From the Dead: The Dynamic Saga of the Chosen People (Atlanta: Hebraic Christian Global Community, 2015), 31-34.
5. Encyclopedia Britannica, ed. Brian Duignan, s.v. "Torah, Sacred Text," Sept. 18, 2019, accessed Oct. 7, 2019, https://www.britannica.com/topic/Torah.
6. Merriam-Webster, s.v. "Tallit," accessed October 7, 2019, https://www.merriam-webster.com/dictionary/tallit.
7. Merriam-Webster, s.v. "Tzitzit," accessed October 7, 2019, https://www.merriam-webster.com/dictionary/tzitzit.
8. Rabbi Abraham Millgram, "The Tallit: Spiritual Significance," *My Jewish Learning*, accessed Oct. 22, 2019, https://www.myjewishlearning.com/article/the-tallit-spiritual-significance/.
9. Strong's H3671, *Blue Letter Bible*, accessed Sept. 30, 2019, https://www.blueletterbible.org/lang/lexicon/lexicon.cfm?strongs=H3671.
10. Noga Tarnopolsky, "The Bible described it as the perfect, pure blue. And then for nearly 2,000 years, everyone forgot what it looked like," *Los Angeles Times*, Sept. 10, 2018, accessed Oct. 7, 2019, https://www.latimes.com/world/la-fg-israel-blue-20180910-html-story.html.
11. Herbert Lockyer, *All the Women of the Bible* (Grand Rapids, MI: Zondervan Publishing House, 1988), 221.
12. Strong's G2899, *Blue Letter Bible*, accessed Oct. 7, 2019, https://www.blueletterbible.org/lang/lexicon/lexicon.cfm?t=kjv&strongs=g2899.
13. Kent Dobson, *NIV First Century Study Bible* (Grand Rapids, MI: Zondervan, 2014), 1,208.
14. Strong's H1697, *Blue Letter Bible*, accessed September 30, 2019, https://www.blueletterbible.org/lang/lexicon/lexicon.cfm?strongs=H1697.

Session Two

1. Encyclopedia Britannica, s.v. "Ecclesiasticus," accessed Oct. 15, 2019, https://www.britannica.com/topic/Ecclesiasticus.
2. Gary Manning Jr., "Good Eye / Bad Eye," Biola University, Feb. 4, 2011, accessed Sept. 30, 2019, https://www.biola.edu/blogs/good-book-blog/2011/good-eye-bad-eye.
3. "Strong's H4941," *Blue Letter Bible*, accessed September 30, 2019, https://www.blueletterbible.org/lang/lexicon/lexicon.cfm?strongs=H4941.
4. Gregory the Great, *Commentary on the Book of Blessed Job*, accessed September 26, 2019, http://faculty.georgetown.edu/jod/texts/moralia1.html.
5. Gerald L. Baum, MD, "L'Chaim!" *JAMA Internal Medicine, Arch Intern Med.*, (August 1979): 921, accessed September 30, 2019, doi:10.1001/archinte.1979.03630450063021.
6. "Strong's H6666," *Blue Letter Bible*, accessed September 30, 2019, https://www.blueletterbible.org/lang/lexicon/lexicon.cfm?strongs=H6666.
7. Strong's H1004, *Blue Letter Bible*, accessed October 8, 2019, https://www.blueletterbible.org/lang/lexicon/lexicon.cfm?strongs=H1004.
8. *Mishnah Middot 1:3, Sefaria*, accessed Nov. 26, 2019, https://www.sefaria.org/Mishnah_Middot.1?lang=bi.
9. Encyclopedia Britannica, Encyclopedia Britannica, eds., s.v. "Mishna," accessed Dec. 2, 2019, https://www.britannica.com/topic/Mishna.
10. Encyclopedia Britannica, Encyclopedia Britannica, eds., s.v. "Judah ha-Nasi," accessed Oct. 8, 2019, https://www.britannica.com/biography/Judah-ha-Nasi.
11. J. E. Bechman, Luis Colina, Hagal Netzer, eds., *The Nearest Active Galaxies* (Dordrecht, Netherlands: Springer Science+Business Media, 1993), 279.
12. Jacob Neusner, ed., *A History of the Mishnaic Law of Purities, Part 15: Niddah: Commentary*, (Eugene, OR: Wipf and Stock Publishers, 1976), I.
13. "14 The Southern Steps and Psalms of Ascent Reminders," *Bible.org*, accessed Oct. 30, 2019, https://bible.org/seriespage/14-southern-steps-and-psalms-ascent-reminders.

14. David Wright, "How Long Were the Israelites in Egypt?", *Answers in Genesis,* July 5, 2010, accessed Oct. 30, 2019, https://answersingenesis.org/bible-questions/how-long-were-the-israelites-in-egypt/.

15. Walter Brueggemann, "The Liturgy of Abundance, the Myth of Scarcity: Consumerism and Religious Life," *Christian Century,* March 24-31, 1999, accessed Nov. 26, 2019, http://therivardreport.com/wp-content/uploads/2016/09/the_liturgy_of_abundance.pdf.

Session Three

1. Encyclopedia Britannica, s.v. "Ecclesiasticus," accessed Oct. 15, 2019, https://www.britannica.com/topic/Ecclesiasticus.

2. Merriam-Webster, s.v. "History and Etymology for cum," "Cum," accessed October 9, 2019, https://www.merriam-webster.com/dictionary/cum.

3. Online Etymology Dictionary, s.v. "em-," accessed Oct. 9, 2019, https://www.etymonline.com/word/em-.

4. Online Etymology Dictionary, s.v. "Pathos," accessed Ot. 9, 2019, https://www.etymonline.com/word/pathos#etymonline_v_10151.

5. *The Didache, 7,* accessed Oct. 15, 2019, http://www.newadvent.org/fathers/0714.htm.

6. Halvor Moxnes, "Honor and Shame," *University of Oslo,* accessed Oct. 30, 2019, https://pdfs.semanticscholar.org/57da/c0eacfcdaa5473f8c-c2185c6fc06be1caa8a.pdf.

7. Charles J. Ellicott, *Elicott's Commentary for English Readers, Vol. 3, John 4:4* (USA: Delmarva Publications, Inc., 2015).

8. Elinoar Bareket, "The Evolution of Biblical Terms through the Ages," *Achva Academic College,* October 2017, Vol. 7, No. 10, 543-552, accessed Oct. 23, 2019, doi: 10.17265/2159-5313/2017.10.004.

9. Strong's H1897, *Blue Letter Bible,* accessed September 30, 2019, https://www.blueletterbible.org/lang/lexicon/lexicon.cfm?t=kjv&strongs=h1897.

10. *God Heard Their Cry Discovery Guide* (Grand Rapids, MI: Zondervan, 2009).

11. "Mount Gerizim and the Samaritans," *United Nations Educational, Scientific and Cultural Organization,* Feb. 2, 2012, accessed Oct. 30, 2019, https://whc.unesco.org/en/tentativelists/5706/.

12. "Temple Ruins Found in Jordan May Be Samaritans' Sanctuary," *New York Times,* Oct. 28, 1964, accessed Nov. 20, 2019, https://www.nytimes.com/1964/10/28/archives/temple-ruins-found-in-jordan-may-be-samaritans-sanctuary.html.

13. Encyclopedia Britannica, Encyclopedia Britannica, eds., s.v. "Mount Gerizim," accessed September 30, 2019, https://www.britannica.com/place/Mount-Gerizim.

14. J.W. McGarvey and Philip Y. Pendleton, *The Fourfold Gospel,* "At Jacob's Well, and at Sychar," via *Bible Study Tools,* accessed Oct. 30, 2019, https://www.biblestudytools.com/commentaries/the-fourfold-gospel/by-sections/at-jacobs-well-and-at-sychar.html.

15. "Mount Gerizim," *Jewish Virtual Library,* accessed Oct. 30, 2019, https://www.jewishvirtuallibrary.org/gerizim-mount.

16. Judah Goldin, Encyclopedia Britannica, s.v. "Hillel," accessed Oct. 29, 2019, https://www.britannica.com/biography/Hillel.

17. Encyclopedia Britannica, s.v. "Shammai ha-Zaken," accessed Oct. 29, 2019, https://www.britannica.com/biography/Shammai-ha-Zaken.

18. "Hillel and Shammai," *Jewish Virtual Library: American-Israeli Cooperative Enterprise,* accessed September 26, 2019, https://www.jewishvirtuallibrary.org/hillel-and-shammai.

19. David L. Turner and Darrell L. Bock, *The Gospel of Matthew - The Gospel of Mark* (Carol Stream: IL, Tyndale House Publishers, 2005), 246.

20. "*Gittin 90a-b: Grounds for Divorce,*" Aleph Society Inc., 2018, accessed September 30, 2019, https://steinsaltz.org/daf/gittin90/.

21. Ibid.

22. Joachim Jeremias, *Jerusalem in the Time of Jesus,* trans. F.H. and C.H. Cave, (USA: SCM Press, 1969), 370.

23. Ibid.

24. Ephrem the Syrian, as quoted by Kenneth E. Bailey, "Jesus and Women," *Jesus Through Middle Eastern Eyes,* (Downers Grove, IL: InterVarsity Press, 2008), 200–216.

Session Four

1. Cyrus Adler and Lewis N. Dembitz, *1906 Jewish Encyclopedia,* , s.v. Parashah, accessed Oct. 15, 2019, http://www.jewishencyclopedia.com/articles/11904-parashah.

2. Moxnes, https://pdfs.semanticscholar.org/57da/c0eacfcdaa5473f8cc2185c6fc06be1caa8a.pdf.

3. Bailey, *Jesus Through Middle Eastern Eyes,* (Downers Grove, IL: InterVarsity Press, 2008) 242-243.

4. Strong's G3850, *Blue Letter Bible,* accessed Oct. 15, 2019, https://www.blueletterbible.org/lang/lexicon/lexicon.cfm?t=kjv&strongs=g3850.

5. Merriam-Webster, s.v. "Parallel," accessed Nov. 20, 2019, https://www.merriam-webster.com/dictionary/parallel.

6. MJL, MJL Admin, "What is the Torah portion?" *My Jewish Learning,* accessed Oct. 30, 2019,

https://www.myjewishlearning.com/article/what-is-the-torah-portion/.

7. Merriam-Webster, s.v. "Parashah," accessed Oct. 23, 2019, https://www.merriam-webster.com/dictionary/parashah.

8. Paul Anthony Chilton, Monika Weronika Kopytowska, eds., *Religion, Language, and the Human Mind*, (New York: Oxford University Press, 2018), 311.

9. Merriam-Webster, s.v. "Parashah," accessed Oct. 23, 2019, https://www.merriam-webster.com/dictionary/parashah.

10. David M. Morgan, ed., *The Weekly Torah Portion: A One-Year Journey Through the Parasha Readings,* (Lake Mary, FL: Charisma House Book Group, 2019).

11. Walter Brueggemann, *From Whom No Secrets Are Hid: Introducing the Psalms* (Louisville, KY: Westminster John Knox Press, 2014), xxiii.

12. Merriam-Webster, s.v. "homo mensura," accessed Oct. 15, 2019, https://www.merriam-webster.com/dictionary/homo%20mensura.

13. Strong's H1980, *Blue Letter Bible*, accessed Oct. 15, 2019, https://www.blueletterbible.org/lang/lexicon/lexicon.cfm?strongs=H1980.

Session Five

1. Charles Spurgeon, *Treasury of David,* Psalm 106:13 (2003), accessed Oct. 25, 2019, from https://app.wordsearchbible.com/reader.

2. Brad H. Young, *The Parables: Jewish Tradition and Christian Interpretation* (Grand Rapids: MI, Baker Academic, 1998), 37.

3. Kenneth E. Bailey, *Finding the Lost* (St. Louis: Concordian, 1992), 97-99.

4. Merriam-Webster, s.v. "Chutzpah," accessed Oct. 16, 2019, https://www.merriam-webster.com/dictionary/chutzpah.

5. Strong's H2142, *Blue Letter Bible,* accessed September 30, 2019, https://www.blueletterbible.org/lang/lexicon/lexicon.cfm?t=kjv&strongs=h2142.

6. Don Stewart, "Why is the Bible Divided into Chapters and Verses?", *Blue Letter Bible*, accessed Oct. 25, 2019, https://www.blueletterbible.org/faq/don_stewart/don_stewart_273.cfm.

7. Kenneth Bailey, *The Cross and the Prodigal: Luke 15 Through the Eyes of Middle Eastern Peasants* (Downers Grove, IL: InterVarsity Press, 2005), 34.

8. N.T. Wright, *Luke for Everyone* (London: Society for Promoting Christian Knowledge, 2001), 187.

Session Six

1. JPost Editorial, "A Timely Celebration," *Jerusalem Post*, Oct. 12, 2019, accessed Oct. 25, 2019, https://www.jpost.com/Opinion/A-timely-celebration-604465/.

2. *Mishnah Shabbat 104b, Sefaria*, accessed Oct. 25, 2019, https://www.sefaria.org/Shabbat.104b?lang=bi.

3. Bruce D. Chilton, *A Galilean Rabbi and His Bible* (Eugene, OR: Wipf and Stock Publishers, 1984).

4. Richard E. Creel, *The Love of Jesus: The Heart of Christianity* (Eugene: OR, Resource Publications, 2010), 26.

5. J. Vernon McGee, *Thru the Bible: Genesis through Revelation* (Nashville, TN: Thomas Nelson, Inc., 1998).

6. Susanna Wesley, *Susanna Wesley: The Complete Writings* (New York: Oxford University Press, 1997), 109.

7. Wayne Stiles, "The Southern Steps and the songs of the High Holidays," *The Jerusalem Post*, Sept. 19, 2011, accessed Oct. 21, 2019, https://www.jpost.com/Travel/Jerusalem/The-Southern-Steps-and-the-songs-of-the-High-Holidays.

8. Earl D. Radmacher, ed., *Nelson's New Illustrated Bible Commentary*, (Nashville, TN: Thomas Nelson, 1999), 1,787.

9. Strong's H8527, *Blue Letter Bible*, accessed Oct. 21, 2019, https://www.blueletterbible.org/lang/lexicon/lexicon.cfm?t=kjv&strongs=h8527.

10. "Being a first century disciple," Bible.org, accessed Oct. 25, 2019, https://bible.org/article/being-first-century-disciple.

11. Thomas L. Friedman, *From Beirut to Jerusalem* (New York: Picador, 2012), 429.

12. Strong's G266, *Blue Letter Bible*, accessed Oct. 22, 2019, https://www.blueletterbible.org/lang/lexicon/lexicon.cfm?t=kjv&strongs=g266.

13. Strong's H3384, *Blue Letter Bible*, accessed Oct. 21, 2019, https://www.blueletterbible.org/lang/lexicon/lexicon.cfm?t=kjv&strongs=h3384.

14. Strong's H7965, *Blue Letter Bible*, accessed Oct. 22, 2019, https://www.blueletterbible.org/lang/lexicon/lexicon.cfm?t=kjv&strongs=h7965.

15. Cornelius Plantinga Jr., *Not the Way It's Supposed to Be* (Grand Rapids, MI: Wm. B. Eerdmans Publishing Co., 1995), 10.

16. Ibid., 5.

17. Susan Schreiner, *Are You Alone Wise?: The Search For Certainty in the Early Modern Era* (New York: Oxford University Press, 2011), 159.

Session Seven

1. Rabbi Ben Bag Bag, as quoted by Ann Spangler and Lois Tverberg, *Sitting at the Feet of Rabbi Jesus* (Grand Rapids, MI: Zondervan, 2017), 25.
2. Moxnes, https://pdfs.semanticscholar.org/57da/c0eacfcdaa5473f8cc2185c6fc06be1caa8a.pdf.
3. John Macarthur, *1 Corinthians New Testament Commentary* (Chicago: Moody publishers, 2003), 355.
4. John MacArthur, *Twelve Extraordinary Women* (Nashville: Thomas Nelson, 2005), 112.
5. Ann Spangler and Lois Tverberg, *Sitting at the Feet of Rabbi Jesus* (Grand Rapids, MI: Zondervan, 2017), 15-19.
6. Ibid., 18.
7. Yose ben Yoezer, as quoted by Spangler and Tverberg, *Sitting at the Feet of Rabbi Jesus*, 11.
8. Deidre Joy Good, ed., *Mariam, the Magdalen, and the Mother*, (Bloomington, IN: Indiana University Press, 2005), 12.
9. "Miriam," *Jewish Virtual Library*, accessed Oct. 30, 2019, https://www.jewishvirtuallibrary.org/miriam.
10. "Mary," *Behind the Name*, accessed September 25, 2019, https://www.behindthename.com/name/mary.
11. "Miriam," *Behind the Name*, accessed Oct. 24, 2019, https://www.behindthename.com/name/miriam.
12. "Ein Kerem," *Bethlehem University*, accessed Oct. 24, 2019, https://www.bethlehem.edu/page.aspx?pid=1435.
13. Noam Dvir, "Ein Karem Under Threat," *Haaretz*, Aug. 25, 2019, accessed Oct. 24, 2019, https://www.haaretz.com/1.5104864.
14. C. S. Lewis, *The Lion, the Witch and the Wardrobe* (New York: Harper Collins, 1978), 196.

Glossary

1. James Orr, ed., *International Standard Bible Encyclopedia*, Bible Study Tools, s.v. "Sirach, Book Of," accessed September 30, 2019, https://www.biblestudytools.com/encyclopedias/isbe/sirach-book-of.html.
2. Ibid.
3. Manning Jr., https://www.biola.edu/blogs/good-book-blog/2011/good-eye-bad-eye.
4. A. Vanlier Hunter, *Biblical Hebrew Workbook* (Lanham, MD: University Press of America, 1988), 69.
5. James Orr, ed., *International Standard Bible Encyclopedia*, Bible Study Tools, s.v. "Stiff-Necked" accessed September 30, 2019, https://www.biblestudytools.com/encyclopedias/isbe/stiff-necked.html.
6. Strong's H1697, *Blue Letter Bible*, accessed September 30, 2019, https://www.blueletterbible.org/lang/lexicon/lexicon.cfm?strongs=H1697.
7. Strong's H1897, *Blue Letter Bible*, accessed September 30, 2019. https://www.blueletterbible.org/lang/lexicon/lexicon.cfm?strongs=H1897.
8. Brueggemann, http://therivardreport.com/wp-content/uploads/2016/09/the_liturgy_of_abundance.pdf.
9. Bareket, "The Evolution of Biblical Terms through the Ages," 543-552, doi: 10.17265/2159-5313/2017.10.004.
10. Strong's H3671, *Blue Letter Bible*, accessed September 30, 2019, https://www.blueletterbible.org/lang/lexicon/lexicon.cfm?strongs=H3671.
11. Baum, 921, doi:10.1001/archinte.1979.03630450063021.
12. Garr, *Life from the Dead: The Dynamic Saga of the Chosen People,* 31-34.
13. MJL, "Why Some Jewish Women Go to the Mikveh Each Month," *My Jewish Learning,* accessed Oct. 29, 2019, https://www.myjewishlearning.com/article/the-laws-of-niddah-taharat-hamishpaha/.
14. Susan Freudenheim, "Becoming Jewish: Tales from the Mikveh," *Jewish Journal,* May 8, 2013, accessed Oct. 29, 2019, https://jewishjournal.com/cover_story/116511/.
15. Jerzy Gawronski and Ranjith Jayasena, "A mid-18th century mikveh unearthed in the Jewish Historical Museum in Amsterdam," *Taylor and Francis Online*, July 19, 2013, accessed Oct. 24, 2019, 213-221, https://www.tandfonline.com/doi/abs/10.1179/174581307X318985.
16. Encyclopedia Britannica, Encyclopedia Britannica, eds., s.v. "Mishna," accessed Dec. 2, 2019, https://www.britannica.com/topic/Mishna.
17. *Pirkei Avot 1:1, Sefaria*, accessed Oct. 29, 2019, https://www.sefaria.org/Pirkei_Avot.1?lang=bi.
18. Strong's G4461, *Blue Letter Bible*, accessed Oct. 29, 2019, https://www.blueletterbible.org/lang/lexicon/lexicon.cfm?t=kjv&strongs=g4461.
19. Nissan HaNasi, "Rabbi Judah the Prince," *Kehot Publication Society,* accessed Oct. 29, 2019, https://www.chabad.org/library/article_cdo/aid/112279/jewish/Rabbi-Judah-the-Prince.htm.
20. J. E. Bechman, Luis Colina, Hagal Netzer, eds., *The Nearest Active Galaxies*, 279.
21. *A History of the Mishnaic Law of Purities, Part 15: Niddah: Commentary,* Jacob Neusner, ed. (Eugene, OR: Wipf and Stock Publishers, 1976), I.
22. Daniel Lynwood Smith, *Into the World of the New Testament* (London: Bloomsbury T&T Clark, 2015), 8.

23. Strong's H4941, *Blue Letter Bible,* accessed Dec. 2, 2019, https://www.blueletterbible.org/lang/lexicon/lexicon.cfm?t=kjv&strongs=h4941.

24. Bailey, *Jesus Through Middle Eastern Eyes,* 203.

25. "At Jacob's Well, and at Sychar," *Bible Study Tools,* accessed Oct. 29, 2019, https://www.biblestudytools.com/commentaries/the-fourfold-gospel/by-sections/at-jacobs-well-and-at-sychar.html.

26. Encyclopedia Britannica, s.v. "Mount Gerizim," Encyclopedia Britannica, eds., accessed September 30, 2019, https://www.britannica.com/place/Mount-Gerizim.

27. Merriam-Webster, s.v. "Parashah," accessed Oct. 23, 2019, https://www.merriam-webster.com/dictionary/parashah.

28. Charlotte Elisheva Fonrobert, "When the Rabbi Weeps: On Reading Gender in Talmudic Aggadah." *Nashim: A Journal of Jewish Women's Studies & Gender Issues 4* (2001): 56-83, https://www.muse.jhu.edu/article/409419.

29. Judah Goldin, Encyclopedia Britannica, s.v. "Hillel," accessed Oct. 29, 2019, https://www.britannica.com/biography/Hillel.

30. Encyclopedia Britannica, s.v. "Shammai ha-Zaken," accessed Oct. 29, 2019, https://www.britannica.com/biography/Shammai-ha-Zaken.

31. *Shabbat 31a, Sefaria,* accessed Oct. 30, 2019, https://www.sefaria.org/Shabbat.31a?lang=bi.

32. *Shabbat 21b:5, Sefaria,* accessed Oct. 30, 2019, https://www.sefaria.org/sheets/89557?lang=bi.

33. Michael Card, *Matthew: The Gospel of Identity* (Downers Grove, IL: InterVarsity Press, 2013), 170.

34. Malka Z. Simkovich, *Discovering Second Temple Literature* (Lincoln: University of Nebraska Press, 2018), 108.

35. Encyclopedia Britannica, s.v. "Septuagint," accessed Oct. 29, 2019, https://www.britannica.com/topic/Septuagint.

36. Merriam-Webster, s.v. "Tallit," accessed September 30, 2019, https://www.merriam-webster.com/dictionary/tallit.

37. Rabbi Jill Jacobs, "Tale of Two Talmuds: Jerusalem and Babylonian," *My Jewish Learning,* accessed Oct. 29, 2019, ttps://www.myjewishlearning.com/article/tale-of-two-talmuds/.

38. Patrick T. Brown, *Embracing Biblical Literacy* (Bloomington, IN: WestBow Press, 2019).

39. Strong's H8451, *Blue Letter Bible,* accessed Oct. 29, 2019, https://www.blueletterbible.org/lang/lexicon/lexicon.cfm?t=kjv&strongs=h8451.

40. "The Tanakh," *Jewish Virtual Library,* accessed Oct. 29, 2019, https://www.jewishvirtuallibrary.org/the-tanakh.

41. Tarnopolsky, "The Bible described it as the perfect, pure blue. And then for nearly 2,000 years, everyone forgot what it looked like," https://www.latimes.com/world/la-fg-israel-blue-20180910-htmlstory.html#.

42. Strong's H6666, *Blue Letter Bible*, accessed Oct. 29, 2019, https://www.blueletterbible.org/lang/lexicon/lexicon.cfm?strongs=H6666.

43. Merriam-Webster, s.v. "Tzitzit," accessed September 30, 2019, https://www.merriam-webster.com/dictionary/tzitzit.

44. Pinchas Shir, "The Fringe of His Garment," *Israel Bible Center,* March 28, 2018, accessed Oct. 30, 2019, https://weekly.israelbiblecenter.com/the-fringe-of-his-garment/.

45. Craig Wagganer, *Simple Lessons Learned Along the Way* (Bloomington, IN: WestBow Press, 2015).

46. Merriam-Webster, s.v. "Yeshiva," accessed September 30, 2019, https://www.merriam-webster.com/dictionary/yeshiva.

47. Strong's H2142, *Blue Letter Bible*, accessed September 30, 2019, https://www.blueletterbible.org/lang/lexicon/lexicon.cfm?t=kjv&strongs=h2142.

48. *Chagigah 9b, Sefaria,* accessed Oct. 29, 2019, https://www.sefaria.org/Chagigah.9b?lang=bi.

Stay in God's Word with studies you're sure to love.

BETTER
By Jen Wilkin
10 Sessions
Study the Book of Hebrews verse by verse to explore how the entirety of Scripture points to Jesus.

lifeway.com/better

GOD OF CREATION
By Jen Wilkin
10 Sessions
Examine the first 11 chapters of Genesis to discover the character, attributes, and promises of God.

lifeway.com/godofcreation

GOD OF COVENANT
By Jen Wilkin
10 Sessions
Delve into Genesis 12–50 to challenge your basic understanding of familiar stories.

lifeway.com/godofcovenant

TRUSTWORTHY
By Lysa TerKeurst
6 Sessions
Study 1 & 2 Kings to learn how to truly trust God.

lifeway.com/trustworthy

FINDING I AM
By Lysa TerKeurst
6 Sessions
Join Lysa TerKeurst on the streets of Israel to explore the seven I AM statements of Jesus found in the Gospel of John.

lifeway.com/findingiam

Lifeway women

Get the most from your study.

IN THIS STUDY, YOU'LL:

- Explore how Jesus generously restores dignity and honor to women in the first century and now
- Gain deeper insight into the biblical world, including fresh perspective on familiar Bible stories
- Discover the Bible through the lens of Middle Eastern culture

Watching Kristi's video teaching sessions is essential to experiencing the full learning impact of the study. Each 60-minute video teaching unpacks fundamental truths and clarifies study questions found in the *Jesus and Women* Bible study book.

STUDYING ON YOUR OWN?

Watch Kristi McLelland's teaching sessions, available via redemption code for individual video-streaming access, printed in this Bible study book.

LEADING A GROUP?

Each group member will need a *Jesus and Women* Bible study book, which includes video access. Because all participants will have access to the video content, you can choose to watch the videos outside of your group meeting if desired. Or, if you're watching together and someone misses a group meeting, they'll have the flexibility to catch up! A DVD set is also available to purchase separately if desired.

Browse study formats, a free session sample, video clips, church promotional materials, and more at

lifeway.com/jesusandwomen

HERE'S YOUR VIDEO ACCESS.

To stream *Jesus and Women* Bible study video teaching sessions, follow these steps:

1. Go to my.lifeway.com/redeem and register or log in to your Lifeway account.

2. Enter this redemption code to gain access to your individual-use video license:

V L K 6 L N 2 D C 9 V L

Once you've entered your personal redemption code, you can stream the video teaching sessions any time from your Digital Media page on my.lifeway.com or watch them via the Lifeway On Demand app on any TV or mobile device via your Lifeway account.

There's no need to enter your code more than once! To watch your streaming videos, just log in to your Lifeway account at my.lifeway.com or watch using the Lifeway On Demand app.

QUESTIONS? WE HAVE ANSWERS!
Visit support.lifeway.com and search "Video Redemption Code" or call our Tech Support Team at 866.627.8553.